D0921731

— ENDORSE.

"God sent Apostle Banks to our ministry in Nigeria at a very critical moment for us. God had instructed me to relocate to another city but continue my oversight of the existing church. The vision was to transition into an apostolic house, opening new campuses, yet operating as one in a healthy interdependence. At the time, we only had a couple of churches in our ministry. Today, we have grown to 21 campuses in 6 nations and counting. The teachings of Apostle Banks have been an integral part of our transition from a local church to a multi-campus house operating with order and harmony. He is always balanced, insightful, and powerful in pulpit delivery as well as on the page. The impact of this book will be deep, far-reaching, and long-lasting on every reader, their local churches, and apostolic networks."

Reverend Victor Adeyemi
Global Lead Pastor
Global Harvest Church Nigeria & Abroad

"Apostle Steven W. Banks challenges and enlightens us as he guides us through the apostolic principles found in the book of Nehemiah. The insight he offers into the biblical truths of the 12 gates is truly illuminating and underscores why he is one of today's leading voices and thinkers in the area of apostolic ministry. One of the most significant relationships that pastors can have is with an apostle who watches and guards the spiritual temperature in their lives. Apostle Banks' voice is much needed in this current and future seasons."

Reggie Stewart
Senior Pastor
International Family Worship Center
New London, Connecticut

"Everyone, my brother Apostle Steven W. Banks has done it again. His latest book Gatekeepers is a must read for transformational leaders in church and in the marketplace. Skillfully using the biblical model of twelve gates from the book of Nehemiah, he stretches us to rethink how we fortify various portals of ministry and life. You will gain invaluable & relevant insights from one of the leading prophetic voices in the kingdom of God. So please, read and grow!"

Dr. John Guns
Dean
Samuel DeWitt Proctor School of Theology at Virginia Union University (VUU)
Richmond, Virginia

"There are some writings that are just on-time and imperative for the Body of Christ and the world at-large; indeed, this is one of them. Apostle Banks brings together the wisdom of experience with the eyes of a father and addresses those areas in the world that desperately need clarity. Reading this book will take you from revelation to practicality. You will get foundational teaching and instruction while learning how we can work together as God's Army to change the world. This reading is for all, believers and non-believers, from leadership to laity."

Pastor David Hawkins
Lead Pastor
Living The Word Church
Collinsville, Illinois

"The shifts occurring in our world right now affirm the need for leadership in every sphere of life by people who have developed Godly character, competence, and capacity. Apostle Steven W. Banks, an apostolic leader with experiences spanning several decades, has provided deep insight and strategies that can move everyone forward in their leadership quotients. This new release, Gatekeepers, will shift your paradigm, equip you to develop the values of Jesus Christ, and empower you to infuse your sphere of influence with those values. I recommend it to everyone conscious of his or her apostolic assignment."

Sam Adeyemi
Senior Pastor
Daystar Christian Centre
Nigeria

"This book is a crucial part of Apostle Steven Banks' assignment in the earth. God has used him as a kingdom scribe to articulate His mind concerning the church and kingdom. Gatekeepers is more than a book; it is a decree and declaration from heaven for the next dimension that God is taking His church into. The insight and revelation of Gatekeepers by Apostle Banks is mandated for this season. This book releases the heart of God for all spheres of ministry and life. Apostle Banks has been my spiritual father and apostolic covering for over 15 years. His wisdom has shifted my life and ministry over the years in ways too innumerable to express. I am excited and honored that he asked me to do an endorsement for this book. The apostolic and prophetic dimension of this book will renew your mind."

Apostle Matthew Tillery
Tri-Faith International Ministries
Rocky Mount, North Carolina

"I have known Apostle Steven W. Banks for over 20 years. In that time, I've discovered him to be a scholar of the Word and one who is always in the forefront of paradigm shifts relative to the kingdom. In his latest release, Apostle Banks unveils a divine revelational download as he skillfully and masterfully weaves a beautiful tapestry that lays the groundwork for all interested in kingdom success and fulfillment in life, ministry, and the marketplace. I believe, to-date, it's his finest masterpiece and a MUST READ!!!"

Bishop Cardinal A. McIntosh
Senior Pastor
Grand Bahama Family Worship Center
Freeport Grand Bahama, Bahamas

"I'm ecstatic about the release of Apostle Steven W. Banks' latest book, Gatekeepers, because the timing has been perfectly orchestrated by God just as the country is re-opening churches following the global pandemic. As we resumed in-person worship gatherings, we must ensure that every component of ministry operates optimally, and this book is instrumental in obtaining that outcome. In Chapter 8, Apostle Banks very eloquently expounds on the selection of individuals appointed to serve in the area of the "Ministry of Helps." The Apostle uses a remarkable comparison of Eve being created from Adam's rib (an inside job) as a suitable model and guideline for our selection process as it relates to appointing individuals to help, aid, and assist with carrying out the vision of the house. In essence, Apostle Banks revealed to us that just as Adam used what was already inside him, we should, likewise, consider utilizing individuals who have been birthed, nurtured, and groomed within our own house to operate in these capacities. This is powerful to me and just one of many profound examples shared throughout this amazing publication that will be used to point leaders to a more excellent way—further advancing the kingdom of God throughout our lives personally, professionally, and ministerially."

Earnest L. Pugh, M. Div, D. Min.
Founder, CEO
Earnest Pugh Worldwide

"When I was connected to Apostle Banks in 2014, as much as I wanted to keep my distance from him, I could not. He carried an anointing that penetrated religious mindsets that I had lived with for years. With a father's concern and love, he began to show me a more excellent and accurate way to do life and ministry. In his new book, Gatekeepers, you will experience the grace of an apostolic father, lending support as you emulate God's original pattern for how the work of ministry should be carried out. The vision God has entrusted to us is too large to manage alone. The good news is that this was never His plan! A place of support is waiting for us to make our arrival. Everything we need is there. It is time to embrace a new and better way. Gatekeepers is not just a game changer it is a life changer."

Dr. Victoria Austin
The Master's Touch International Outreach Ministries
Milton, Florida

"Apostle Steven Banks has been a consistent and reliable voice that God has used to shape the consciousness of kingdom leadership for decades. Gatekeepers is evidence that God has selected him to be a clarion voice in such a critical time in the history of our world. This book establishes the foundations of faith and expresses the importance of aligning ourselves with biblical patterns so that we can gain Godly outcomes. We are privileged to be made privy to the mind of God through the pen of Apostle Banks. I was enriched and empowered by this robust read. I am certain that you will concur once you've turned the last page."

Bishop Ronald L Godbee Sr.
Lead Pastor
The River Church
Durham, North Carolina

"Apostle Banks places emphasis on key areas of growth and an understanding that will assist all readers in obtaining a solid foundation of what makes up a healthy apostolic ministry. As churches embrace the five-fold ministry there is a need for biblical and sound teaching on critical apostolic principles. This book is not only good for apostolic leaders, but also their congregation and those unfamiliar with the mantle of an apostle."

Apostle Mike Hathaway
Lead Pastor
New Generation Church
Richmond, Virginia

"Simply amazing… Apostle Steven Banks writing style is precise, powerful, and persuasive! Gatekeepers is a must read for anybody seeking spiritual growth in an apostolic setting. Therein he profoundly declares, "it is impossible to get into the new dimension by yourself" and "without any spiritual help and helpers, you may never walk into higher dimensions of the spiritual realm."

Apostle William M. Dawson
Senior Pastor
Mount Gilead Baptist Church
Williamsburg, Virginia

"Apostle Steven Banks has masterfully bridged the gap between the text and the times, as his passion and pen have kissed to bring us Gatekeepers. Like the sons of Issachar who knew the times and what course to take, this work unlocks kingdom direction for ministry and marketplace influence. Not only has Apostle Banks' ministry impacted me since my childhood days in my father's church, but I also remain awed by his relevance, revelation, and apostolic resilience to feed and lead this generation. As you digest this book, you will not merely read the words of wisdom found therein; you will encounter the worth and work attached to the journey this General in the faith has taken to produce it. As Nehemiah's gates granted physical access, may this journey usher you into heavenly places. "

Rev. Cedric D. Rouson, M.Div.
Lead Pastor
Shekinah Kingdom Church
Chesapeake, Virginia

"Apostle Banks has written yet another masterpiece! This thought-provoking guide is great for anyone in ministry serving in all capacities. This book can easily be used as a manual to take you to the next level spiritually. Get ready for an outpour of revelation."

Pastor Fred Wyatt
Speaking Spirit Ministries
Richmond, Virginia

"Gatekeepers by Apostle Steven Banks is an incredibly thoughtful, unique, and special gift written to help the body of Christ and the world at-large. The masterfully written content is very relatable, encouraging, and easy to understand. It will both empower and educate you. As a Senior Pastor, this book moved me with its practical and personal insights on how to relate to each of the apostolic centers in both the church and the marketplace. Definitely a must read! I would highly encourage those in a leadership position to get more than one copy of this amazing book and share it with everyone they work with and lead."

Edwin E Strickland
Senior Pastor
Fellowship of Champions Church International
Fayetteville, Arkansas

"I was blown away by the insight of Gatekeepers! The skillful way in which Apostle Steven Banks introduces and guides the reader through level after level of fresh information and revelations places him in the company of the leading visionaries of our day. This book is especially relevant for the challenging times that we are living through and speaks prophetically to any and all seeking to achieve a higher level of knowledge, relationship, and spirituality in life in general. Pastors, ministers, church leaders, and servants at all levels will appreciate information that will fortify their ministries in new and exciting ways. Gatekeepers is a must have addition to any legitimate library."

Pastor Paul S. Pleasants
Calvary Baptist Church
Saluda, Virginia

"God has changed the landscape of ministry and marketplace ministry with this revelation from Apostle Banks. Every ministry & kingdom business professional, along with social entrepreneurs who represent the Global consciousness of the Lord Jesus Christ should not only read, but systematically apply the information released therein. This is not just good reading material; this is a tool. One that can be used for every season of the ministry leader or kingdom professional. From evangelism, to lifestyle, to finance and family, Apostle Banks equips the believer with a treasure of resources to build legacy with a solid foundation. What a wonderful piece of technology you're holding in your hand in the form of a book."

Apostle Steven J. Newton Sr.
The Kingdom Center Global
Quantum Technologies
Shreveport, Louisiana

"Gatekeepers by Apostle Steven W. Banks is a relevant kingdom tool for current and evolving leaders. Having been impacted by the ministry of Apostle Banks for over 30 years, I can attest to his consistent voice of clarity, releasing timely insight and instructions for growth. This publication serves as an extension of all that he has deposited into my life. Moving from the concept of religion and realizing the importance of kingdom relationship is fundamental. Apostle Steve shares regarding the 12 gates of Nehemiah and transformational keys in the areas of apostolic order in the church, para-ministries, and the marketplace. If you're ready to be empowered with kingdom truth, you'll invest in purchasing this publication for yourself, your ministry, business, or organization."

Apostle Valerie Burrell
Empowerment Place Ministries
Bluefield, WV

"Simply stated, Gatekeepers is a masterpiece crafted in the crucible of wisdom and revelation. Apostle Banks has poured so much into this labor of love, and it is a MUST READ! The scriptures remind us that we have thousands of teachers but not many fathers, somehow Apostle Banks seamlessly operates as a teacher with the heart of a true apostolic father. I pray this book will find its way into the hands and the hearts of current and emerging leaders in both the kingdom and the marketplace."

Apostle Kevin Mihlfeld
Washington, DC

"As a Spiritual daughter, since 2002, I am honored to know Apostle Steven W. Banks and call him "Dad". Through the years, I have watched, learned, and greatly benefited from the apostolic mantle and prophetic grace that freely flows from his life. This great leader of leaders is a standard-bearer indeed, and his life-changing ministry clearly establishes the requirement of character, integrity, sacrifice, obedience, and worship unto God; and the reward given to those who live in the realm of the Gatekeeper!"

Prophet Iko Blackmon
Author of *Beat The Devil Runnin'*
Atlanta, Georgia

"Steven W. Banks, a 21st century apostle, is a kingdom giant, apostolic father, and a trusted international voice. His most recent book, Gatekeepers, reflects the heartbeat of God. This timely and relevant book is reflective of Apostle Banks' time in communion with God to share His desire for order and clear, practical understanding of the role and function of the Apostolic gift to the church.

There is no one else who could articulate the heart of God with the clarity and precision of Apostle Banks. His study and years of experience, both in spiritual and secular realms, as a leader, allow him to make priceless deposits in the hearts of hearers and readers alike. Allow the words of this book, the revelation of the Spirit, and the heart of this leader to minister to you and usher you into greater understanding of the Gatekeeper."

Bishop Darryl J. McClary, Sr.
Senior Pastor
New Light Church
Chesapeake, Virginia

"This prolific international speaker, Apostle Steven W. Banks, author of Gatekeepers, demonstrates the purpose of the Gates of Nehemiah with profound eloquence. Taking nothing for granted in the biblical text surrounding each gate, Apostle Banks gives us a microscopic view of every gate's purpose. While each chapter of Gatekeepers is enlightening, the revelation aligned with Nehemiah 3:28, "Beyond the Horse Gate the priests made repairs, each in front of his own house" was riveting as he expresses the necessity of the ministry of helps. I highly recommend Gatekeepers for senior leaders as a training resource to build an effective ministry team! Apostle Steven W. Banks' work over the decades is admirable, now the world has access to what makes a mega-mogul-mind like his so successful through Gatekeepers. We appreciate the apostolic legacy and gift to the world in the form of Steven W. Banks!"

Apostle Tim Harrell, Sr,
Senior Executive Leader
Rebirth Community Church, Inc.
Tim Harrell Global Leadership, Inc.
Norfolk, Virginia

"Apostle Steven Banks is a general of revelation and a well of wisdom. Gatekeepers offers fresh insight for apostolic leaders and apostolic types concerning our assignment to man the gates of our regions, territories, industries, and nations. The information is invaluable, and the impartation is eternal. Get ready to be upgraded in your mantle accoutrements and expressions."

Dr. Dwayne Whitehead II
Lead Pastor
The Destiny Center RVA

"When I think of the term, gatekeepers, I can't help but think of Apostle Steven W. Banks. He is the pioneer of my apostolic understanding and awareness. I am amazed at how he was able to go into the scriptures and pull out these 12 Gates and use each one of them to enlighten us on the nature and characteristics of apostolic leadership. Of all the chapters, my personal favorite is chapter three dealing with the Old Gate. In this chapter, Apostle Banks addresses a sensitive subject dealing with maturity in leadership. He explores maturity from an angle that causes us to grow beyond old stale and mundane traditions and beliefs, and he implores us to train and develop modern day, mature leaders in ministry, business, and family. When you read this book, you will want to meet the author. He is simply brilliant!"

Apostle Charlie B. Ammons
General Overseer
Restoration Covenant Alliance International (RCAI)

"Apostle Steven W. Banks is in step and in tune with what the Holy Spirit is saying today. Gatekeepers is a timely, prophetic treatise and instruction manual to inform and equip church and parachurch leaders and marketplace ministries on how to be effective and experience good success. Apostle Banks takes both a pragmatic and spiritual approach as he uses practical examples to explain spiritual principles. Steven W. Banks continues to be a leading prophetic voice that God uses to release and introduce the Body of Christ to new spiritual technology that is sure to make kingdom-building more manageable and productive. Congratulations to Apostle Banks on yet another masterful scholarly work."

Pastor Dexter Howard
President and Senior Pastor
Howard International Ministries
The Restoration Place Church

GATEKEEPERS

A RELATIONAL APPROACH

GATEKEEPERS
A RELATIONAL APPROACH

by
STEVEN W. BANKS

KINGDOM RULE
PUBLISHING
WWW.KINGDOMRULE.COM

A division of Consuming Fire Incorporated
WWW.CONSUMINGFIREINC.COM

ATLANTA, GEORGIA

Published by Kingdom Rule Publishing, a subsidiary of Consuming Fire Incorporated.

Kingdom Rule Nonfiction.

Kingdom Rule Publishing
508 Whaley's Lake Dr, Jonesboro, GA 3028

Kingdom Rule Publishing is a subsidiary of Consuming Fire Incorporated
Visit our website at www.consumingfireinc.com

Printed in the United States of America

First Kingdom Rule Publishing Printing: September 2021
ISBN: 9798490407232

Photo by Tonya D. Mitchell
Cover design by Stephen Blackmon.

− *Dedication* −

My growth as a spiritual father is a direct result of the greatest privilege, joy and honor that I have in the world, being called "dad" by two of the most amazing people on the planet. Keira Iman and Jordan Imanuel, please know that I am released because you two have released me to soar.

— *Acknowledgements* —

I am forever grateful to one of the most amazing teams ever assembled. Each one of you have provided not only your phenomenal skills, but your hearts. May you take pleasure in knowing that the Kingdom of God is being impacted as a result of your tireless dedication to this assignment. With great joy I salute and honor each of you.

Robin Holland, Editor
Rebecca Phillips, Editor
John Conley, Editor
Sandra Hughes Smith, Consultant
Tonya D. Mitchell, Photographer
Stephen Blackmon & Consuming Fire Inc.

Special thanks and gratitude to a tremendous kingdom leader, coach and friend, Apostle Stephen J. Newton and The Kingdom Center Global team.

— CONTENTS —

— Introduction —

As many of you know I was blessed to release and publish a book in 2007 titled *Apostolic Gatekeepers*. My study of the twelve gates of Jerusalem and the associated principles of leadership illustrated in this book began over two decades ago. I've been studying leadership nearly all my life, and in that book, I got the opportunity to use the 12 gates to convey some of these concepts utilizing a biblical perspective.

A lot has happened since 2007. I've been pastoring and leading men and women in one form or another since my early twenties and much has changed in the last 15 years. The world has changed; MY world has changed. My God, and my love for Him have not. His goodness has not, and His principles of leadership have not. I've written this book because my understanding of His Gates, His principles, and how to lead from a healthy, balanced, effective, and sustainable perspective has grown considerably. My understanding of how to establish oneself as a leader who can endure the storm and make a greater transformational impact has grown. This additional knowledge merited the expansion of what I'd previously taught.

This new book, *Gatekeepers,* allows me to use my experiences, personally and ministerially, to readdress these pillars needed to function effectively as leaders (whether in ministry or marketplace) from a place of greater experience, transparency, and vulnerability. Each one of these pillars, contains insights that can be utilized to make our churches, businesses, families, and personal lives healthier. While *Gatekeepers* maintains its structural foundation, this venture shifts an intense focus onto relationships. Many have order, yet a minimal understanding of the significance of relationships. We all must do better and be intentionally relational as we provide leadership to the various visions that have been entrusted to us.

Over the years, both publicly and privately, I have experienced great successes and profound challenges and losses. It has been an amazing journey and I am truly grateful for every phase, season, and circumstance. Nevertheless, I know that my God saves the best for last. *Gatekeepers* uses my journey to grant you unique access into seasoned "apostolic ministry". This will give you invaluable insight to help you carry out the calling on your own life, while providing you the capacity to instruct others.

I am an apostle. I am male. I am African-American. These are some of the primary parameters and perspectives from which I live and write. I have been wired genetically and distinctively for this assignment. Having been involved in both traditional and non-traditional ministry locally and globally, I have had the humbling opportunity of serving as a trailblazer in "apostolic ministry." I am honored to be on the cusp of providing leadership to those venturing into new realms of ministry, business, and life.

Most of the context for this discussion is drawn from church or ministry, however the applications apply equally to those who desire to provide skillful and excellent leadership in the marketplace. This book is for those who are serious about establishing and enhancing their ministries, businesses, and personal lives through providing meaningful care to the relationships and organization(s) that you have been privileged to lead.

I encourage you to allow the Holy Spirit to minister to you through the words, the heart, and the testimony of all I discuss, and take it far beyond merely what is written on these pages. May this enlighten and inspire you with an overwhelming passion to develop and to expand yourself, your relationships, and your organizations for His glory!

CHAPTER 1

The Sheep Gate

THE PLACE OF REPENTANCE AND SALVATION

"Then Eliashib the high priest rose up with his brethren the priests and built the Sheep Gate; they consecrated it and hung its doors. They built as far as the Tower of the Hundred, and consecrated it, then as far as the Tower of Hananel."

Nehemiah 3:1

In order to better comprehend the foundation and significance of the Sheep Gate, we must first understand the many customs, traditions, and the culture of Jerusalem for this time. Sheep were an important and vital part of the possessions and wealth of the ancient Hebrew people and of most eastern nations. Sheep were of great benefit and purpose in those times. Perhaps most importantly, they were used as sacrificial offerings in the tabernacle. This would signify why the Sheep Gate was the first gate to be restored. This gate led to the sheep market where the sacrificial lambs were bought and sold. The Sheep Gate not only denotes restoration, but it also represents Salvation. Prophetically, the Sheep Gate is symbolic of Christ as the Lamb of God and the cross.

"He was oppressed and He was afflicted, Yet He opened not His mouth; He was led as a lamb to the slaughter, And as a sheep before its shearers is silent, So He opened not His mouth."

Isaiah 53:7

When Jesus went to Golgotha, He came out of and through the Sheep Gate.

"...Behold! The Lamb of God who takes away the sin of the world!"

John 1:29

It was Nehemiah's assignment to ensure the gates were restored, but it was a high priest by the name of Eliashib, along with his brethren, who rebuilt the Sheep Gate. What is interesting is that the name Eliashib means "to return to or to turn back to", which indicates restoration. There was a reason God prioritized the Sheep Gate's restoration. God is reminding us that the first thing that we must do is to restore our relationship with Him, and this is accomplished through the Lamb of God.

UNDERSTANDING REPENTANCE

God desires our repentance and is longsuffering in an effort to afford humanity the opportunity to return to Him. That is the place of authority. The essence of the gospel is rooted in the Book of John:

"For God so loved the world that He gave His only begotten Son, that whoever believes in Him should not perish but have everlasting life."

John 3:16

Regardless of how trendy the church becomes; it is essential that personal salvation remains a cornerstone experience. We have all fallen short of God's glory and it is through the gracious act of repenting that we find our way into a trusting relationship with Him.

Repenting is not only a change of mind, but it is a change of purpose and direction. It is the act of returning to the High Place; the restoration of relationship and fellowship with God. In the American Dictionary of the English Language, 1828, Noah Webster defines Repentance like this:

a) A change of mind, or a conversion from sin to God.

b) The relinquishment of any practice, from conviction that it has offended God.

There is a correlation and a connection that we all must have in the House of God: We have to make sure that our ministries, our teachings, and everything that we do in the House of God is rooted and grounded in finding the "highest place" possible. That is the penthouse. It is the elevated place. We must ensure that the people coming into the House of God are first coming in through the Gate of Salvation, and then, establishing a relationship with God through the power of repentance.

THE DOCTRINE OF CHRIST

"Therefore, leaving the discussion of the elementary principles of Christ, let us go on to perfection, not laying again the foundation of repentance from dead works and of faith toward God, of the doctrine of baptisms, of laying on of hands, of resurrection of the dead, and of eternal judgment."

Hebrews 6:1-2

These principles are referred to as the Doctrine of Christ. They are foundational, and elementary. The first doctrine is repentance from dead works. Even before the doctrine of faith towards Him, God wants to make sure that we lay the foundation of repentance properly and in order. Repentance deals with the individual mindset. A properly laid foundation of repentance will be manifested in the way one thinks and the actions one displays from those thoughts.

"And the peace of God, which surpasses all understanding, will guard your hearts and minds through Christ Jesus. Finally, brethren, whatever things are true, whatever things are noble, whatever things are just, whatever things are pure, whatever things are lovely, whatever things are of good report, if there is any virtue and if there is anything praiseworthy—meditate on these things. The things which you learned and received and heard and saw in me, these do, and the God of peace will be with you."

Philippians 4:7-9

A mind that's focused upon operating in high places has to intentionally be focused upon thoughts that are true, honor, just, pure and lovely.

> "...*whatever things are true, whatever things are noble, whatever things are just, whatever things are pure, whatever things are lovely, whatever things are of good report, if there is any virtue and if there is anything praiseworthy—meditate on these things.*"
>
> *Philippians 4:8*

A Christ-like mind will focus on thoughts of good report and dismiss negative thoughts. Understand the process; thoughts trigger feelings – feelings trigger actions – and actions build character. Your character defines your being.

MANIFESTING THE KINGDOM OF GOD

Faith towards God is the second foundational principle we must apply. In the simplest of terms, before you go to the second grade, you must complete the first grade. Before you go to college, you must complete high school. Before you do anything in Christ, you must first begin with laying the foundation of repentance. The foundation has to be laid and set. A building can only stand firm and stable if it has been built on a strong foundation. Many people call themselves mature in the things of God, but are relying and operating on a faulty foundation. If the foundation is faulty and not rooted in the Word of God, then the house will sink.

"Therefore, leaving the discussion of the elementary principles of Christ, let us go on to perfection, not laying again the foundation of repentance from dead works and of faith toward God,"

Hebrews 6:1

The word "perfection" as stated in Hebrew 6:1 signifies spiritual maturity. It is not the will of God for the church to stay in an infant stage. The city will never see the Glory of God through an infant church. Your family will never see the Glory of God through a baby believer. It is time for the church to grow up and mature in the ways of God. Before you start serving God or doing anything in His name, you need to make sure that you have properly laid the foundation of repentance and faith in your life.

In all of our preaching and our teaching, we are called, foremost, to lift up our Lord Jesus Christ – His birth, life, death and the resurrection. This is what my homiletic professor; Dr. Miles Jones called the "kerygmatic content". We need to make sure that our houses are rooted in the foundation of salvation through repentance. The foundation is the most important part of the house and it must be solid. Naturally, if you attempt to build a house on a faulty foundation, the house will not stand. Likewise, in the body of Christ, the same principle applies. The foundation of the Word and repentance must be solidified first. I enjoy mentoring leaders, as well as functioning in the capacity of a life coach. These are pivotal assignments within the Kingdom of God, but when we talk about an Apostolic House of God, the motivation is the cross! We all need inspirations and motivation along our journey. Fortunately, there are a plethora of individuals who are gifted to help motivate us through their subject mastery, yet the Holy Spirit is the life giving force in our lives not only to inspire us, but also to anoint us to execute the assignment.

"From that time Jesus began to preach, and to say, 'Repent: for the kingdom of heaven is at hand.'"

Matthew 4:17

The Kingdom of God will never be manifested without the foundation of repentance. You will have a House that is a social club with social order, but not Kingdom operation. In the Book of Joel, the Word of God declares that in the last days, He will pour out His Spirit on all flesh.

"And it shall come to pass afterward that I will pour out My Spirit on all flesh; Your sons and your daughters shall prophesy, Your old men shall dream dreams, Your young men shall see visions."

Joel 2:28

I believe that we are in the midst of the greatest outpour of the Holy Spirit that this world has ever seen. Many are not able to discern the time because they are trying to understand it with their carnal mind, which is light-years behind the spirit man. If you are trying to interpret the Word of God by using your carnal mind, you will be confused and in doubt. That is why you need to let the Holy Ghost lead you into the truth. This is not the time for the church to be weak and confused. This is not the time for you to give up! This is the time of Elijah - the time of miracles, revival and of restoration. These are the last days and the set time for your sons and daughters to be saved, baptized, and filled with the Holy Ghost.

RESTORATION THROUGH REPENTANCE AND CONFESSION

> *"Repent therefore and be converted, that your sins may be blotted out, so that times of refreshing may come from the presence of the Lord, and that He may send Jesus Christ, who was preached to you before, whom heaven must receive until the times of restoration of all things, which God has spoken by the mouth of all His holy prophets since the world began."*
>
> *Acts 3:19-21*

Where there is no repentance, there will be no refreshing. We need houses that are fresh and will refresh those who are weary and depleted! We need a fresh wind of God to breathe anew over our lives. I do not want yesterday's manna; every new day, I want fresh manna. Understand this,

> *"Heaven must receive him until the time comes for God to restore everything,..."*
>
> *Acts 3:21 NIV*

God is saying, "I have to hold my Son back." I am ready to release Him, but I cannot release Him until the time comes for God to restore everything.

Some things are out of alignment; out of order. God is saying to His people that it is time for restoration. He is ready to restore relationships. He is ready to restore Five-Fold Ministry to the House of God and restore the manifestation of healing, miracles and signs. God is saying before Jesus comes back, He has to restore. It is restoration time! Understand that God is restoring not some things, but ALL things.

The church of the living God has been out of order for way too long, governmentally. So many churches are governed by democracy. People literally vote on everything, from the selection of the carpet to the selection of and often the firing of the pastor. I have been fortunate to pastor in denominational and non-denominational churches, as well as being exposed to various denominations and reformations. Church structure and governance is at the root of many of the issues within the Body of Christ. Since we live in a democracy here in America, there are those who believe that the church should be governed by democratic principles. It is possible for the direction of the church to be dictated solely by a majority vote. Need I remind you, the majority never thought they could take possession of the Promised Land.

I have pastored in churches under this type of government. One thing that was amazing in this context was that, individuals were drawn to the church because of the anointing that was being released during the services. However, very few were aware of the warfare that was taking place behind the scenes during the week. I recall "officials of the church" calling me into meetings to address things such as my attire (not wearing robes), to the length of my messages, to my leadership style, and everything else that you can imagine. This escalated to the point of having harassing, anonymous letters mailed to my house from an "ad hoc" committee, largely composed of the church officers' spouses. Yet in this toxic environment, there was no space allowed for council from overseers (bishops, apostles, etc.) or even wise and seasoned pastors.

As we go further in this writing, we will deal specifically with leadership structure and functions within the local congregations, as well as within the corporate body as a whole. The church of The Living God is a living, breathing, evolving organism to which Jesus, The Head of The Church said,

> "...on this rock I will build My church, and the gates of Hades shall not prevail against it."
>
> *Matthew 16:18*

Above all, the church is The House of God, The Gate of Heaven. Its structure and function is that of a Kingdom, not a democracy. It is a spiritual called-out assembly, not a social club governed by ordinates and dictates as if it were a fraternity or sorority.

One of the wisest and safest things for a pastor to do is to intimately engage in relationships with seasoned and mature leaders who have been proven in ministry and in life. The counsel and support offered by these mature people will be lifesaving and will greater advance pastors, their relationships and their ministry.

For so long we have looked at Jesus confronting Nicodemus and commanding him to be born again as a directive for personal conversion, and it is. However, Nicodemus represents the greater "religious system" that needs to be converted. He is a ruler/leader of the religious establishment and he teaches within that context. That "religious system" must be born again, due to its toxic nature. It engulfs individuals into formalities that over time will deplete the very essence of life from them. That "system" will reduce individuals to living solely by letter and laws as opposed to love. That "system" will be hierarchical in its principles and in its practices, where one is valued, and placed based upon their racial, social and/or economic pedigree. So, as opposed to being an agent of liberation, the "system" has become a blatant vehicle of oppression for those who are not a part of the status quo.

The Sheep Gate is the portal of entry into the Kingdom of God, for the individual and for the system. It is the Sheep Gate where we graciously ask for God's love to forgive us for attempting to make His Church our house. It is here where we repent from relying upon our abilities, ideas and passions. How grateful we are for all that have been entrusted to us, to have stewardship of our lives and along our journey. However, repentance yields our very best to the Blood of Calvary's Redeemer,

"...all our righteous acts are like filthy rags;..."

Isaiah 64:6

Repentance is turning away from the dependency on ourselves and the systems that we have created. We lay everything down at His feet, totally and completely, trusting Him to use any and all of it for His Glory.

FELLOWSHIP WITH GOD

"If we say that we have fellowship with Him, and walk in darkness, we lie and do not practice the truth. But if we walk in the light as He is in the light, we have fellowship with one another, and the blood of Jesus Christ His Son cleanses us from all sin. If we say that we have no sin, we deceive ourselves, and the truth is not in us. If we confess our sins, He is faithful and just to forgive us our sins and to cleanse us from all unrighteousness. If we say that we have not sinned, we make Him a liar, and His word is not in us."

I John 1:6-10

You must be in fellowship with Him. Anytime we walk in darkness and sin is rampant in our lives, we are out of fellowship with God. Repentance does not stop at salvation. It is not just something you do to be saved, but it is an ongoing process in the heart of the believer. There are areas in our lives where God is shining the light on and exposing the darkness. He is giving us an opportunity to make it right with Him. Where there is unconfessed sin, God is unable to show Himself mighty in your life. The believer's confession should be, not if, but when you find anything in my life that is not of you, purge it out.

Confessing is an acknowledgment of missing the mark. The downfalls within the faith community are being revealed and uncovered to show us that we are not to put our salvation and trust in man. There will always be a parade of fleshly activity, not spiritual movement, when sin is unexposed in the church. Yet and still, God is faithful. He is faithful and just to forgive us of our sins and to cleanse us from all unrighteousness when we confess our sins.

"If we confess our sins, He is faithful and just to forgive us our sins and to cleanse us from all unrighteousness."

I John 1:9

As long as you are alive, you will never get to the place of perfection. There will always be things on the inside of each of us that God wants and needs to deal with. If you do not allow Him to deal with you one-on-one, He may have to send a Nathan to you with a prophetic word. He will do this, not to harm or shame you, but because of His faithfulness and unending love towards you. In the book of II Samuel, God had to send Nathan to David to let him know that even though he was a man after God's heart and loved to worship Him, he had not repented of his sin. David knew that he was wrong for coveting Bathsheba, another man's wife. Instead of repenting and confessing his sin to God, he compounded the wrong he had done. He did this by first sleeping with her and then sending her husband, Uriah, to the front line of a fierce battle so that he would be killed.

"Then the men of the city came out and fought with Joab. And some of the people of the servants of David fell; and Uriah the Hittite died also."

II Samuel 11:17

As if that was not enough, he then took Bathsheba as his wife. Unconfessed sin will cause you to sink deeper and deeper into unrighteousness and will draw you further away from the presence, the will and the heart of God. It is a dangerous and dark hole.

Where there is no repentance, the spirit man on the inside of us begins to decay. We begin to walk in condemnation, bondage, guilt and shame. The enemy will have a stronghold on you and will continually speak negatively into your life. However, where there is repentance there will be a joyful sound, because you are making it right with the Lord. You will experience freedom, newness, liberty, and no condemnation from Him who loves you. The presence of God will begin to be removed from your life if you do not repent. Whatever you do, you do not want the Lord to take His Holy Spirit away from you.

"Do not cast me away from Your presence, And do not take Your Holy Spirit from me."

Psalm 51:11

Not only do we sin with our bodies, but we also miss His mark with our thoughts, by being envious, jealous and bitter within our hearts and mind towards others. As an apostolic leader, your desire should always be to lift holy hands and have a clean heart so that God can work mightily in your life. However, when there are things in your life that do not reflect the heart and will of God, do not expect Him to overlook that. He is such a loving God that He knows the things in your life that will hinder your growth.

Whenever you realize that you have missed the will of God, you need to go before Him to ask for His forgiveness. You need to seek God immediately when you notice that you have allowed something to pull you away from Him. When you recognize that there is something keeping you from your destiny, the only thing you can do is ask God to forgive you. There should be no pride, but humility in going to the Father with a broken and contrite spirit. God is not moved or impressed by our talents, abilities or resume, but a pure and broken heart moves God. Has your heart been broken before the Lord? Are you sensitive to the heart of God? Never allow pride to get so comfortable in your life that you can knowingly sin and it does not bother you. I am scared of people who have no regard for sin. The Word of God teaches us to reverence Him and to fear Him. Some people may say that this does not mean to be scared of God, but just to have reverence for Him. There is something called the 'Fear of the Lord'. He alone has the titles of Almighty and All Powerful and I just do not play with God. There should be things that you simply just will not allow because of the fear of the Lord.

As gatekeepers, we understand that the foundation of our lives is built on repentance. Repentance is coming back to God and asking God for forgiveness. This is a continuous lifestyle. It is our desire as believers that God continually renew within us a right spirit and a clean heart. If you ever get to the point where you can commit sin and totally disregard your treatment of others and have no remorse over it, then you are in a dangerous place. The more mature we become, the more we understand what God is trying to do in our lives. He teaches us to first deal with our own shortcomings before we find any sin and fault in someone else's life. The Amplified Bible says:

"Why do you see the speck that is in your brother's eye but do not notice or consider the beam [of timber] that is in your own eye?"

Luke 6:41 Amp

Finally, as apostolic people we have been commissioned to be the light of the world. The Word of God declares,

"...A city that is set on a hill cannot be hidden."

Matthew 5:14

The presence of His Glory upon your life should be a ray of hope and inspiration to those who dealing with darkness. We are greatly encouraged by the prophetic word of Isaiah,

"Arise, shine; For your light has come! And the glory of the Lord is risen upon you. For behold, the darkness shall cover the earth, And deep darkness the people; But the Lord will arise over you, And His glory will be seen upon you. The Gentiles shall come to your light, And kings to the brightness of your rising."

Isaiah 60:1-3

We exist in the midst of a world reeling from the devastation of the COVID-19 pandemic that has taken the lives of over 600,000 individuals in America and over 4,500,000 worldwide while still climbing daily. Similar to the Great Depression, we face a severe economic crisis with the closure of businesses, both large and small, as well as unemployment rates at the highest seen since the 1930's.

In addition to the health and economic crises we are facing, there has been a growing resurgence of racism. A boiling point came when we witnessed the televised murder of George Floyd.

An officer placed his knee upon Floyd's neck for 8 minutes and 46 seconds (8:46). The surrounding officers assisted in either holding Floyd down or did absolutely nothing while this Black man cried out for his deceased mother between proclamations of, "I can't breathe!" George Floyd's murder resulted in marches and protests not only nationally, but globally.

These are truly unprecedented times in history; unlike any we have seen before. Yet and still, it seems that Isaiah's prophetic and poetic words have been set into motion where he speaks about a gross darkness covering the earth. He discerns the environment and atmosphere; however, Isaiah also releases a word of great hope and victory declaring that, "The Lord rises upon you and His glory shall appear over you". With such vigor and hope, he boldly charges the people of God to arise and shine in the midst of darkness for their light has come. This is a declaration for manifestation. Darkness, even gross darkness shall not prevent the manifestation of God's glory upon His creation. For all of creation is at full attention waiting for those who are graced and prepared to be released in their kingdom authority to execute their assignment in the earth realm. This is the decade where the intent of God releasing you into the earth realm shall be manifested. It shall not be revealed in the midst of light but in the midst of darkness, gross darkness.

This releasing will take place as we turn from our plans, thoughts and ways, to allow Him to elevate us into the high places. As we enter in through repentance and have a total reliance upon Him. The sheep gate ushers us into this experience.

CHAPTER

The Fish Gate

THE PLACE OF OBEDIENCE AND DISCIPLINE

"The Fish Gate was rebuilt by the sons of Hassenaah. They laid its beams and put its doors and bolts and bars in place."

Nehemiah 3:6

"And as He walked by the Sea of Galilee, He saw Simon and Andrew his brother casting a net into the sea; for they were fishermen. Then Jesus said to them, "Follow Me, and I will make you become fishers of men." They immediately left their nets and followed Him."

Mark 1:16-18

STEPPING OUT OF THE BOAT

The Fish Gate represents obedience and discipline. It is at this gate that training and teaching are paramount. This is the chief aim. Discipline must be taught and rehearsed; soldiers are taught discipline in basic training and rehearse it daily, because it undergirds their entire military career. For many people, simply hearing the words obedience and discipline sparks recoil because it carries a negative connotation. However, building a victorious life upon God's Word requires us to obey His Word and to exercise discipline in our lives.

God is a God of order, and therefore requires us to follow the patterns that He is setting forth. As new structures and paradigms are emerging, He will require an exchange to occur in order to move us to our next dimension. One must be willing to relinquish their reliance and familiarity with current structures, systems, and mindsets that they have operated in for years in order to enter through these new and exciting portals. For most, it will be extremely challenging because too few have been wired to think critically, and even fewer still have been able to envision new realities and modalities. An uncharted realm is a courageous endeavor to venture into when one has been comfortable in that which has been familiar for so long.

In some cases, these structures have served their purpose and usefulness. In other cases, they have been restrictive and have prohibited fresh, creative growth from occurring. It is the same with many of us today. We want new truth, we seek out and attempt to be committed to new truth; however, we are hesitant, or in most cases flat out refuse to release the old truths, even after they have been found to be inaccurate.

An exchange must take place for us to encounter greater heights and deeper depths in our journey with God. We do a great disservice to ourselves and to our assignment when we become so dogmatic and defensive in attempting to uphold our thoughts without having any inquisitive inclinations. We have been admonished to remain seekers or life-long learners. That is where discipline and obedience step in. We have arrived at various stations in life, yet as we venture forward, we need proceeding words, as described in the Book of Matthew, to propel us into new realities.

"But He answered and said, "It is written, 'Man shall not live by bread alone, but by every word that proceeds from the mouth of God.'"

Matthew 4:4

At this juncture, we are positioning ourselves to learning and knowing His voice. There must be a keen awareness and sensitivity to His Spirit when He speaks. Not only have you been equipped to know the written Word, but you have also matriculated in the teachings of the Spirit of God. It is simply not enough to know His Word and to stop there, for Paul stated,

"… not of the letter, but of the spirit: for the letter kills, but the spirit gives life."

II Corinthians 3:6

Unfortunately, staying solely at the level of the letter will often times only produce death, judgment, and legalism.

You could not imagine having an active soldier serving in battle who is not obedient and disciplined. The danger this individual poses to themselves, those serving alongside them, the larger community, and the nation as a whole is immeasurable. Winning the battle hinges on them obeying the rules and adhering to the discipline of their training.

Obedience has a direct correlation to one's understanding of authority and needs to be cultivated within the hearts of believers. Building on the apostolic foundations of God's Word, requires us to fully trust His Word and to be disciplined in our lives. As previously stated, God is a God of order and requires us to follow the patterns and directions that He has and is setting forth. In establishing new and fresh structures, we must be willing to detach from preconceptions of how ministry and life should look, feel, and function. Being relevant is pivotal and that will necessitate a great sensitivity to His Spirit as He unfolds His pattern for you as opposed to simply recreating what you have been accustomed to. New structures may have some similarity to previous versions, however our faith must be pliable enough to stretch and fit to the unfolding of His Spirit. Therefore, obedience is imperative, He says to the prophet Isaiah,

"Behold, I will do a new thing, Now it shall spring forth; Shall you not know it? I will even make a road in the wilderness and rivers in the desert."

Isaiah 43:19

So we must accept and embrace that these are new and uncharted territories that we must explore and experience.

One of the major functions within apostolic centers is to equip the saints for the work of the ministry. These apostolic centers –

churches, hubs, businesses, agencies – must be laser-focused on the training and preparation of those entrusted to their jurisdiction. We are commissioned to make fishers of men. Once the people come into the Sheep Gate, they must now undergo a disciplining process. Teaching is a major way of equipping individuals, especially in a progressively diverse and sophisticated culture where people are transient, such as in a densely populated military area.

For example, there were some major focal points that I taught several times each year, such as spiritual warfare, prayer, the fivefold ministry, finance, and forgiveness. These were some of the foundational teachings that my ministry members heard consistently throughout the year. Since teaching was a major thread within my ministry, we developed The Center for Leadership Development. This was a way to develop various pathways to allow members to seek greater depth in various subject matter. Apostolic centers must be rooted in and committed to teaching as a training vehicle.

Those within leadership must not only ensure that they sharpen the tools they have been given, but also that they develop the ability to relate to and be engaged with people gracefully and authentically. For example, individuals who operate their own businesses are taught that their business is an apostolic center, and they are not solely positioned for financial gain, but they are entrusted in the development of those who work and serve in that business. The business owners are not merely sharpening their professional skills, but also their excellence, integrity, and intelligence to represent the Kingdom of God in the marketplace.

Teaching brings clarity to your vision and to those who are connected to your assignment. The word "apostolic" has different meanings to different people. For some, it refers to a denomination, just like other Christian denominations, such as Baptist, Methodist, or Church of God in Christ. For others, apostolic refers to a baptismal formula, where one is baptized in Jesus' name as opposed to being baptized in The Name of the Father, Son and Holy Ghost. Still, for others, it may refer to the code of attire that women wear representing "modest apparel". All of these, as well as various other meanings are applicable in their given context.

When I use the term apostolic, I am specifically referring to a dimension of ministry and life that is derived from the Book of Ephesians, as well as other significant passages.

"And He Himself gave some to be apostles, some prophets, some evangelists, and some pastors and teachers,"

Ephesians 4:11

Within this dimension or realm, there is a mindset, an anointing, a grace, and gifting that uniquely operates through those who are wired to function from this perspective. This apostolic realm consists of, among other things, an anointing for trailblazing, pioneering, governing, establishing and releasing. Truly apostolic centers create and cultivate environments that release the liberty and movement necessary for those who are apostolically wired to thrive. These centers foster internal and external relationships that will aid in the activation of those who are connected.

In order for us to become fishers of men, we must allow

His word to deal with us as we are being prepared. We must be taught. Disciples are not simply made through preaching; they are developed through teaching. Before we are commissioned to represent the heart and mind of God, we must commit ourselves to the sound teachings. A skilled fisherman knows what equipment to use and the proper time to use it. A fisherman understands the environment in which they are fishing, as well as the most beneficial time to fish. There are major differences between recreational and professional fishermen, largely due to the training. Professionals have learned much, but are continuously learning and looking for ways to perfect their craft.

"Come to Me, all you who labor and are heavy laden, and I will give you rest. Take My yoke upon you and learn from Me,..."
Matthew 11:28-29

Before released to provide leadership within any organization, you must be developed. An undeveloped/underdeveloped leader carries the potential to bring great harm and pain to themselves as well as to many others. God desires to make you a disciple. He is concerned about the process, not just our outcome. We must give diligent care to the process as well as the outcome. We are refined in the process. Your processing is going to prepare and cultivate you to be released. The execution of Kingdom principles will determine the length, magnitude, and growth of your process. The detailed instructions are what you will need to get through the process and progress to your specific and intended assignment.

DISCIPLESHIP

"Then Jesus said to those Jews who believed Him, "If you abide in My word, you are My disciples indeed."

John 8:31

Discipleship is not an effortless process. It challenges your endeavor to learn the ways of God through submission, worship, studying, meditating, and living the Word. Discipleship is the everyday practice and lifestyle of the believer. It involves every aspect of your life and being. It is so much larger than church attendance, since it is a continuous work of learning to rely on His Word and the leading of His Spirit. Church attendance is the tip of the iceberg. A disciple understands the importance of daily discipleship as needed to propel them to their destiny. A disciple will come to the understanding that, to know Him is to learn Him, love Him, and serve Him. Membership focuses largely upon weekly attendance; discipleship focuses upon daily development and is exhibited in relationships with one's family, business, and place of employment; all aspects of life. The sole aim of discipleship is to bring your soul into alignment with your Kingdom assignment. This enables you to add others to the Kingdom because of winning your own soul.

POSSESSING YOUR SOUL

"By your patience possess your souls."

Luke 21:19

The soul consists of three parts—the mind, the will, and the emotions. It is the task of each individual to attend to the development and training of the soul. Detailed attention has to be given to disciplining of the soul or else a person becomes extremely susceptible to the devices of the enemy.

Having gone through the Sheep Gate of repentance and conversion, we become new creatures in Christ. We have experienced the personal salvation of our spirit solely by the grace of God. We have entered into a relationship with God whereby we are born of His spirit and now our spirit has direct access to our Heavenly Father; this is the part of our being that is God-conscious because of our rebirth.

Now, spiritually, we are seated together in heavenly places because we have received God's greatest gift into our hearts, His Son. As beautiful as this experience is, there is still work that we must do individually. I will never forget the day that I personally received Him into my life on March 16, 1981 at a Christian rock and roll concert in Mathews, Virginia. As a high school athlete, I was introduced to the Lord through the Fellowship of Christian Athletes.

Yet, I had no idea that the inner work was just starting according to the book of Philippians,

"…work out your own salvation with fear and trembling."

Philippians 2:12

This referred to my soul, attending to my mind, my will, and my emotions. This has been a daily journey from that day forward, and will be until the Lord calls me home.

As we have given the Lord our hearts, we now must undergo rigorous training to bring our soul into alignment with His will for our lives. The battleground, for the most part, is the arena of our minds. We have been taught, consciously and even subconsciously, beliefs and thought patterns that are contrary to His Word. He confronts our mindset directly with His Word.

"For My thoughts are not your thoughts, Nor are your ways My ways," says the Lord.

"For as the heavens are higher than the earth, So are My ways higher than your ways,

And My thoughts than your thoughts. "For as the rain comes down, and the snow from heaven, And do not return there, But water the earth, And make it bring forth and bud,

That it may give seed to the sower And bread to the eater, So shall My word be that goes forth from My mouth; It shall not return to Me void, But it shall accomplish what I please,

And it shall prosper in the thing for which I sent it."

Isaiah 55:8-11

The training and retraining of our soul requires a constant focus on the Word of God in our lives that will elevate our thinking so that we develop the mind of Christ. Paul described it as the renewing of our minds. It is paramount for our minds to come into agreement with God's thoughts and plans for our lives. This will result in us having to re-think and to re-imagine our lives, systems, and structures from God's perspective and not based upon the lens that has been utilized in our prior experiences or lack thereof. We must allow His Word to address the mental strongholds that have been erected throughout our lives. Training the mind is a major internal re-working of the soul that we all must undergo.

Mastery of our will is pivotal in carrying out His assignment for our lives. When dealing with His temptations, Jesus responded,

"...the spirit indeed is willing, but the flesh is weak."

Matthew 26:41

There will always be battles raging in our soul between our spirit, which desires to please the Father, and our flesh, which desires to please the father of lies. We see the anguish and the agony that Jesus dealt with personally in the garden of Gethsemane when He prayed saying,

"Father, if it is Your will, take this cup away from Me; nevertheless, not My will, but Yours, be done."

Luke 22:42

The decision rested solely in His will to choose to follow the will of God or the following of His weary and worn flesh. One of the most confrontational encounters is recorded in the synoptic gospels – (Matthew, Mark & Luke), where Jesus is tempted of the devil three times after He had fasted 40 days and nights.

Jesus was at His weakest posture, both physically and emotionally, yet being so determined in His will, responded each time with His allegiance to live by the Word and not by His natural needs. Therefore, discipline is imperative within our souls because there are moments and seasons when we all become weary and weak. It is in these moments that our discipline comes to our aid. When our will is out of alignment, we simply become defenseless.

The last aspect of our soul that we must continuously address is our emotions. We are created as emotional beings; however, we should not allow our emotions to govern us. Most of the pains that we deal with can be categorized as soul wounds, from rejection, betrayal, anger, insecurity, and abandonment, to grief. Feelings are an intricate part of the healing journey, as they are where the authentic anointing of God is released upon our lives; it is the crushing of the olive that produces the oil. Life has a way of causing great pain. We feel the blows of shattered dreams, broken relationships, and major disappointments, but we cannot afford to let these hurts go unaddressed in our lives. Suppressing the emotions tied to these events is extremely unhealthy. These traumas and unprocessed wounds will become the "root of bitterness" that will eventually spring up and cause you great trouble. Too often in ministry, leaders focus on identifying the 'beam' within others while neglecting their own issues.

A leader's perspective is skewed when their 'beams' are not properly dealt with. We must do the soul-based work within our emotional lives, so that we are not bleeding on others because of our untreated wounds. The unprocessed wounds become the excess weight that is slowing us down from hitting our targets and fulfilling our promise.

Jesus, 'the sacrificial Lamb' is described in the Book of Isaiah as,

"...despised and rejected by men, A Man of sorrows and acquainted with grief..."

Isaiah 53:3

As a result of the emotional pain He experienced on earth, He can now be "touched with the feelings of our infirmities." We all experience emotional pain and challenges, but we cannot allow these wounds to direct our lives. As the Wounded Healer, Jesus graciously comforts us on our healing journey. Emotional healing is layered and requires the penetrating, yet gentle work of the Holy Spirit to unearth some pains, patterns, and limiting beliefs that have been operating in our lives for years, whether knowingly or unknowingly. The healing of the soul requires yielding before the Lord. I strongly recommend individuals to receive professional therapeutic help to understand the unique genetic and emotional wiring of your life based upon many variables. Some of the variables include upbringing, parental relationships, living environment, education, religious exposure, economic background, and racial and gender identity just to name a few. Every variable will affect who you are today and how you respond to situations. As you discipline (possess) your soul, it will allow your will, mind, and emotions to respond according to His Word instead of responding from a place of brokenness or hurt.

CHAPTER

The Old Gate

THE PLACE OF FOUNDATIONAL MATURITY

"Moreover Jehoiada the son of Paseah and Meshullam the son of Besodeiah repaired the Old Gate; they laid its beams and hung its doors, with its bolts and bars."

Nehemiah 3:6

LEADERSHIP

The Old Gate typifies two things. First, the Old Gate represents the Eldership within the city. In particular, it represents the mature and seasoned leaders within the House.

"Her husband is known in the gates, When he sits among the elders of the land."

Proverbs 31:23

During biblical times, this gate was the place where business transactions took place. The elders would sit at the Old Gate planning and issuing judgment and discernment for the City.

People who passed the Old Gate recognized the seasoned leaders and acknowledged their ability to release judgment and provide counsel.

The Old Gate is not representative of one's age, but rather of one's maturity in life and in the things of God. An individual can be mature in age or years, but still be an infant in the Spirit. The fact is, your maturity is not measured by how old you are, but by how you have matriculated in the school of the Holy Ghost. When you mature in the things of God, you are no longer considered a child of God, but a Son of God. Sonship, in the scriptures, refers to the continuous growth and maturity of the believer. Keep in mind, even the "matured" believer has not arrived, but is still in a process of growing. As long as you are alive on this earth, you will never arrive, but you are maturing as you strive daily to grow in His ways. The Apostle Paul stated,

"I press toward the goal for the prize of the upward call of God in Christ Jesus."

Philippians 3:14

When we read Proverbs 31, we typically focus on the specific attributes of the virtuous woman; however, one of the attributes mentioned is the integrity and honor that her husband possessed. He is an asset to her and not a liability. According to verse 23 of this chapter, her husband is known in the gates, when he sits among the elders of the land. Her husband's maturity in the city contributes to her virtue and righteousness. He is a decision maker in the community. He is not a simple man, but one that is seasoned, matured, and qualified to deal with and discuss the weighty matters pertaining to the community.

The Old Gate is where mature individuals are raised and released into leadership. One of the pastoral tasks is to train-up and oversee the development of leaders who will be accepted, acknowledged, and respected by the flock as the set authority over them. These leaders will have the heart of the set man/woman of God and will also walk in the same spiritual anointing. Immature leaders are incapable of providing quality leadership acumen to aid in the development of others.

THE APPOINTMENT OF LEADERS

"And so it was, on the next day, that Moses sat to judge the people; and the people stood before Moses from morning until evening. So when Moses' father-in-law saw all that he did for the people, he said, "What is this thing that you are doing for the people? Why do you alone sit, and all the people stand before you from morning until evening?"

And Moses said to his father-in-law, "Because the people come to me to inquire of God. When they have a difficulty, they come to me, and I judge between one and another; and I make known the statutes of God and His laws."

So Moses' father-in-law said to him, "The thing that you do is not good. Both you and these people who are with you will surely wear yourselves out. For this thing is too much for you; you

*are not able to perform it by yourself. Listen now to my voice;
I will give you counsel, and God will be with you: Stand before
God for the people, so that you may bring the difficulties to God.
And you shall teach them the statutes and the laws, and show
them the way in which they must walk and the work they must
do. Moreover you shall select from all the people able men, such
as fear God, men of truth, hating covetousness; and place such
over them to be rulers of thousands, rulers of hundreds, rulers of
fifties, and rulers of tens. And let them judge the people at all
times. Then it will be that every great matter they shall bring
to you, but every small matter they themselves shall judge. So it
will be easier for you, for they will bear the burden with you. If
you do this thing, and God so commands you, then you will be
able to endure, and all this people will also go to their place in
peace."*

*So Moses heeded the voice of his father-in-law and did all that
he had said. And Moses chose able men out of all Israel, and
made them heads over the people: rulers of thousands, rulers of
hundreds, rulers of fifties, and rulers of tens. So they judged the
people at all times; the hard cases they brought to Moses, but they
judged every small case themselves."*

Exodus 18:13-26

This text is often referred to as the Jethro Principle. The Jethro
Principle addresses several aspects of leadership including, healthy
relationships, wise counsel, oversight, and delegation of authority.
This principle has been a major model for me and my ministry

over the years, regardless of the service I provided, whether serving as pastor, bishop, or apostle.

Jethro is a man of relationships. His value for relationships is seen through the tender and compassionate care that he offers to Moses. Jethro was personally invested in Moses. It is Moses, the set-man, who is attending to the daily affairs of Israel. We see how engaging the relationship was between these two. Their love and honor were reciprocal. This was not a one-sided relationship but was a mutually beneficial one. Moses' meeting with Jethro and his bowing and kissing him was an act of reverence and respect. After hearing the testimony of how God delivered Moses, we sense the equal admiration Jethro has for his son-in-law.

Jethro also displays his love and concern for the children of Israel by his keen insight into preventing their weariness, teaching, and instructing them (verse 20) and in empowering them through delegation. This is fatherly wisdom in demonstration, desiring for the best of the total body, not just for the "set man". Even though he does not have an intimate relationship with each one of the children of Israel, he is personally engaged in their wellbeing and release for ministry.

A subtle nuance, often overlooked, is the fact that Jethro is equally concerned about Zipporah. She may not be as visible as Moses is in this text, yet the reason Jethro is there rests largely in the fact that she is his daughter. Jethro is a loving father and is equally concerned that his daughter is being properly cared for by her husband. As Moses is the leader of this nation, Jethro's insight and voice reminds us of Moses' role as a husband, so that he is properly caring for and nurturing his wife. Jethro perceived that as long as Moses was busy from morning until evening that Zipporah was not being properly cared for.

Moses' pattern of leadership was that he was the "set man" and that he was responsible for taking care of the children of Israel individually, while at the same time neglecting that level of care for his wife. As long as the people were getting their needs met, they were in great shape and this pattern of ministry would have continued as long as they would live. With the enormous weight of leadership upon Moses, it is probable that when he was home that he was there physically, but not emotionally. In my book *Healing the Father Wound*, I especially address fathers who may be physically present yet emotionally unavailable. There are distinct reasons why they may be emotionally unavailable or distant. Due to Moses' demands and stress levels, we can easily conclude that he was fatigued.

The number of spouses and preacher's kids that have grown up with deep seated resentment and bitterness toward ministry is countless. This is primarily because ministry took precedent over their relationships with their spouses and parents. Yet, no one in this entire account talked to Moses to encourage him to shift the template of ministry, except for Jethro. Moses felt the burden! Zipporah and the children felt the burden! The children of Israel felt the burden! Fortunately, Jethro's insight added years to Moses' life and greater liberty to his marriage and his sons, Gershom and Eleazer.

Jethro, which means excellence, provided much-needed insight and counsel. Listed below are some apostolic functions that will aid us today just as Jethro aided Moses in his day.

1. Went to the Place of Ministry - (*verse 5*)

   There are some things that can only be observed within the actual place of ministry. There are some nuances that cannot be conveyed by ministerial reports sent to "headquarters" monthly, quarterly, or annually. Reporting is a needed part of oversight; however, some things must be observed in their context in order to be accurately discussed. This observation is best conducted during the regular operations of the ministry, not during special services or events.

2. Heard the Heart of Those He Ministered To - (*verse 8*)

   So often in ministry, communication is one-sided. Truly little dialogue takes place. Moses shares with Jethro about his hardships, as well as all the wonderful works the Lord did. Jethro did not show up with any agenda other than to share with them through the ministry of his presence. As much as I enjoy ministering, there are times when I love to simply visit; not just for a church service, but to spend quality time together. I desire that my presence will be as weighty as my words.

3. Shared with Those He Ministered To - (*verses 9-12*)

   This was a time where Jethro merely came to fellowship

and revel in God's faithfulness with the people. Jethro went to celebrate and he brought an offering. This was not about Jethro; this was about Moses! There are times when fathers need to bless their children. I have been fortunate to have the opportunities to bless many who refer to me as their "Spiritual Father" materially, spiritually, as well as financially with no expectation of a return, other than their betterment.

4. Discerned the Situation - (*verse 14*)

Discernment, or lack thereof, will either release you to another realm or restrict you to the natural. Jethro's discernment was extremely sharp, yet his true mastery was in how he voiced his concern. The skillful way he asked Moses "what is this thing that you are doing?" postured the way he would provide council. Had Moses responded from an egotistic or narcissistic perspective, Jethro would have known to address whether Moses had the right intent in serving the people. Had Moses responded as if he was the only one who could speak into the issues, that would have been an indication of attitude or ego. We can tell by the way Moses responded to the question that his heart was right and that he was not operating out of an inflated sense of self-importance, rather that he was simply unaware.

5. Accessed the Situation - (*verses 17-18*)

Apostolic Gifts are readily able to discern and access situations in an instant. Oftentimes, apostle's schedules require moving and traveling from one location to another. Therefore, discernment must be sharp and accurate at all times. One moment, one word, one encounter with an apostle can shift you and everyone connected to you.

6. Offered Godly Counsel – (*verses 19-23*)

As one who is seasoned in ministry and in life, Jethro knew the value of his own words. Even though this was a unique situation for Moses, Jethro was not moved nor intimidated by the enormity of these conditions. His wisdom was weighty because over the years, Jethro had encountered some challenging things within ministry and within life. It came to the surface as a significant issue for Moses during this time, yet confronting this situation was not difficult at all for Jethro. He was pre-wired for this in his makeup. Had this been outside of his metron or sphere of operation, then he would have had to summon others for counsel and insight. This was not even a stretch for him.

Moses himself was not above taking counsel even though he was a man in a position of authority and power. Moses not only listened to the advice of Jethro, but also implemented it. Fragile leadership would not have responded this way nor this quickly. Unhealthy leadership would have been intimidated and defensive.

Look at how quickly Moses responded to counsel by selecting qualified leaders.

In order to execute ministry with excellence, Moses was instructed to select individuals with the following traits;

1. Capable
2. God fearing
3. Lovers of truth
4. Not engaging in covetousness

Once Moses found such men, he was instructed to make them rulers of thousands, rulers of hundreds, rulers of fifty, and rulers of ten. The significance in assigning some thousands, some hundreds, some fifty, and some ten is called the measure of rule. When you operate in your measure of rule, you can speak into situations that are under your authority and impart counsel, wisdom, and insight. When you operate in your measure, you are demonstrating maturity. A mature leader will recognize when an issue is beyond their measure (over their head). They will be able to discern and know when a thing is too weighty for them to handle, bear, or endure. Egotistical leaders often operate beyond their measure in an attempt to "prove" themselves.

The leaders or rulers that Moses chose were to handle the smaller cases, but any matter outside their measure, they were to bring to him. Moses would be able to spend more time seeking the wisdom and counsel of the Lord now that help, and the measure of rule had been established and implemented. This would enable him to release revelation to the people under the anointing.

This is the same concept prescribed for today's churches. Shepherds are called to find able men (and women) in our congregations that meet these same qualifications. We are to train them and release them in the House to assist in the spiritual matters of the House.

WOMEN IN MINISTRY

"Then God said, "Let Us make man in Our image, according to Our likeness; let them have dominion over the fish of the sea, over the birds of the air, and over the cattle, over all the earth and over every creeping thing that creeps on the earth." So God created man in His own image; in the image of God He created him; male and female He created them. Then God blessed them, and God said to them, "Be fruitful and multiply; fill the earth and subdue it; have dominion over the fish of the sea, over the birds of the air, and over every living thing that moves on the earth."

Genesis 1:26-28

It is important to discuss women in ministry while we are here at the Old Gate. The scripture says God gave Adam and Eve equal authority. He blessed them both male and female. Yet we find in the modern-day church the inequity of women and the distorted and imbalanced headship that says only men can rule. One of the greatest challenges that we all confront is sexism within the church. Misogyny is running rampant in our society and within many church bodies. However, when you study the scriptures, you find Paul saying in Philippians

"... help these women who labored with me in the gospel, with Clement also, and the rest of my fellow workers, whose names are in the Book of Life."

Philippians 4:3

These women were not just responsible for menial tasks, but they were co-laborers in the preaching of the gospel. Historically, we have seen some women become recognized in the ministerial offices of Evangelist and Prophets. More recently we are witnessing women serving in the pastoral ministry. Even more recently we are now seeing women providing leadership within the ministerial of Apostles. The anointing knows no gender. However church history has been extremely sexist and misogynistic.

The Word of the Lord says,

"There is neither Jew nor Greek, there is neither slave nor free, there is neither male nor female; for you are all one in Christ Jesus."

Galatians 3:28

We see this verse dealing with three elements:

1. There is neither Jew nor Greek (dealing with racial preference)

2. There is neither bond nor free (dealing with social/economic preference)

3. There is neither male nor female (dealing with gender preference)

When dealing with individuals from various backgrounds, Jesus was always aware of the person's ethnicity and social experience, as well as their gender. While there was always recognition, preference was neither given, nor denied based on these factors.

In Ephesians, the Word says,

"When He ascended on high, He led captivity captive, And gave gifts to men."''

Ephesians 4:8

This term "men" in this context comes from the term "Anthropos", which is the root word for anthropology. Anthropology is the study of humanity, which includes both male and female. It is not dealing with a male only exclusive fraternity. The Word continues,

"And He Himself gave some to be apostles, some prophets, some evangelists, and some pastors and teachers, for the equipping of the saints for the work of ministry, for the edifying of the body of Christ,"

Ephesians 4:11-12

The word "some" refers to male and female:
1. some to be apostles (both male and female)
2. some prophets (both male and female)
3. some evangelists (both male and female)
4. some pastors and teachers (both male and female)

The anointing knows no gender! Let us take a look at just a few examples of women leaders in the Bible.

OLD TESTAMENT – WOMEN IN MINISTRY

"So Hilkiah the priest, Ahikam, Achbor, Shaphan, and Asaiah went to Huldah the prophetess, the wife of Shallum the son of Tikvah, the son of Harhas, keeper of the wardrobe. (She dwelt in Jerusalem in the Second Quarter.) And they spoke with her."

II Kings 22:14

Though not immediately recognized, we see a prophetess named Huldah. According to the scripture, she lived in Jerusalem. The Priest and several other men of God sought her out for counsel. No doubt she was a learned woman of influence and wisdom, for even the priests desired to consult and fellowship with her. Some theologians believe that she was not just a teacher but a scholar who taught Jewish women as well as men.

In Exodus 15:20, Miriam the prophetess, the sister of Aaron, took a timbrel in her hand and all the women went out after her with timbrels and with dances. Miriam was a worship leader and a prophetess. Micah the prophet refers to her as one of the triumvirate leaders (Moses, Aaron and Miriam) God used to deliver Israel from Egyptian bondage. She led the Israelites with Moses and Aaron.

"For I brought you up from the land of Egypt, I redeemed you from the house of bondage; And I sent before you Moses, Aaron,

and Miriam."

Micah 6:4

In Judges 4:4, we find Deborah, who is a prophetess, the wife of Lapidoth, and a judge over Israel. Deborah served in the highest authority and order in the land at that time. She ranked with the likes of Sampson and Gideon.

These are examples of women who not only served alongside men in the ministry, but they were also appointed and anointed leaders who served over regions.

NEW TESTAMENT – WOMEN IN MINISTRY

In Romans, the Apostle Paul writes to the church at Rome,

"For I long to see you, that I may impart to you some spiritual gift, so that you may be established—"

Romans 1:11

What was this spiritual gift that he wanted to impart? I believe the Spiritual Gift he wanted to impart was that of a Pastor. The vessel he chose was a woman named Phoebe. In Romans, Paul writes about Phoebe again. He says,

"I commend to you Phoebe our sister, who is a servant of the church in Cenchrea, that you may receive her in the Lord in a manner worthy of the saints, and assist her in whatever business she has need of you; for indeed she has been a helper of many and of myself also."

Romans 16:1-2

He then adds,

"Greet Priscilla and Aquila, my fellow workers in Christ Jesus,"

Romans 16:3

This was a gifted husband and wife team. Priscilla was an equal partner with Aquilla and was ordained by God for ministry just as he was. Remember, again, the anointing knows no gender!

As Paul continues to extend greetings, he mentions another apostolic couple, Andronicus and Junia. He further refers to them as his kinsmen, and fellow prisoners. Paul goes further in identifying them, not just as relatives (whether physically or spiritually), but as noted among the apostles. He is saying that they were exceptional apostles, even becoming apostles before himself. In this chapter, Paul specifically named ten women who were a part of his apostolic team. As stated by Paul, Junia was an exceptional apostle who was a woman. Unfortunately, over the last 600-700 years Bible translators and commentators have translated Junia's name into a male name Junias. However, early on it was known and accepted as Junia.

Throughout God's Word we see God using available and open vessels, both men and women. At this Old Gate (seasoned and mature) we see a prophetic snapshot of what the end time church will look and sound like. He says in Joel,

"And it shall come to pass afterward That I will pour out My Spirit on all flesh; Your sons and your daughters shall prophesy, Your old men shall dream dreams, Your young men shall see visions."

Joel 2:28

The text decrees in the last days your sons and daughters will prophesy. It is not restricted to traditional myths concerning women in leadership, but is inclusive of males and females, as well as the young and the old serving in ministry. We see throughout the Word that God does not prohibit women in ministry.

ESTABLISHING THE FOUNDATION

The teaching of doctrine takes place at the Old Gate. Our charge is to be diligent and faithful in teaching the Word of God. What we must immediately take notice of is the current attack on the Old Gate; the attack on sound biblical doctrine. Foundational doctrines are pivotal in our lives. Throughout history there have been movements that have blatantly attacked the doctrine of the Word and the kerygma; (the birth, life, death, and resurrection of Jesus Christ). These movements have come to pollute and to attempt to shake the foundation of the people of God.

Jesus asked his disciples the question, "Who do men say that I am?" They answered, "John the Baptist; Elias, and one of the prophets." Then he asked them, "Who do you say that I am?" Peter immediately responded, "Thou art the Christ, the Son of the Living God." Jesus, the Son of the Living God, declares to Thomas, "If you have seen me, you've seen the Father."

Secondly, the Old Gate signifies that which is growing old. It represents a lack of energy, strength and vitality. This lack of energy, strength and vitality is due to attention deficit, inattentiveness, and other distractions. We have failed to give attention to numerous foundational issues within the apostolic centers because those things are now considered impractical and irrelevant. The mindset has become that we should no longer deal with them because they are no longer of significance.

> *"And they sang responsively, praising and giving thanks to the Lord: "For He is good, For His mercy endures forever toward Israel." Then all the people shouted with a great shout, when they praised the Lord, because the foundation of the house of the Lord was laid."*
>
> *Ezra 3:11*

The Ezra text helps us to see that the people of God rejoiced and praised God, not when the steeple went up, but when the foundation was laid. It is at the Old Gate where the foundation of sound and healthy doctrine must be established. If the doctrine of the Word of God is not properly laid or properly attended to, then the people of God will become weak.

In the Book of Psalms, a question is asked,

> *"If the foundations are destroyed, what can the righteous do?"*
>
> *Psalm 11:3*

The exterior of the House of God may have a towering steeple, contain rich mahogany pews, and have many beautiful stained glass windows, but what is the foundation built upon? Take a look at your own life. It may glitter and look good on the outside, but what's going on inside of you? What is the foundation of your life? What are you building upon or centered around?

A foundation takes longer to build than the house itself. You may have instructed the contractor to build you a house and months later you return only to see he has gotten no further than the foundation. The foundation takes the longest because it is the most important part of the house; it is what will stabilize the house and allow it to stand firmly against the winds, rains, and storms that will arise.

Jeremiah is a prototype of an apostolic prophet. He was called and anointed to:

"...root out and to pull down, To destroy and to throw down, To build and to plant."

Jeremiah 1:10

The function of the apostolic assignment is to infiltrate cities, regions, and nations; to tear down the order and establishments of the kingdom of darkness. The order of God can only be built after the disorder is torn down and discarded. This foundation must become the pillars, roots, and strength of the apostolic ministries. There is a lot of glitz and glamour to Christianity today, but dare I to say to you, "what glitters is not always gold". There are many fads and trends sweeping our churches, however, the foundation must be carefully examined to establish that its roots are firmly planted in sound Biblical doctrine. By examining the foundation, we can ensure that our houses are not built on sinking sand and subject to failure. Because the enemy does not desire to lose any more territory, he attacks the foundation of the house. This is the reason doctrine is under such concentrated attack in these last days.

In Chapter One, we lifted up Hebrews 6:1-2 and its reference to the doctrine of the foundation of Christ. Now let us look at another reference.

FOUNDATIONAL ROOTS

"Then those who gladly received his word were baptized; and that day about three thousand souls were added to them. And they continued steadfastly in the apostles' doctrine and fellowship, in the breaking of bread, and in prayers. Then fear came upon every soul, and many wonders and signs were done through the apostles."

Acts 2:41–43

Take note of this! The church is growing. About 3,000 were added to the church that day and they continued steadfastly in the apostles' doctrine. This is where the roots were established and planted. They stayed steadfast in the apostles' doctrines; the teachings of apostles, who themselves were rooted and walking upright with God. These were individuals filled and led by the Spirit. There will never be signs and wonders if the root is not established accordingly to the Word of God.

Remember, I said the Old Gate represents the lack of energy, strength and vitality. God is saying in these last days that He needs people that are willing and able to rebuild the House of the Lord. He is looking for men and women who will make sure that the House contains an Old Gate.

"But you must continue in the things which you have learned

*and been assured of, knowing from whom you have learned
them, and that from childhood you have known the Holy Scriptures, which are able to make you wise for salvation through
faith which is in Christ Jesus. All Scripture is given by inspiration of God, and is profitable for doctrine, for reproof, for cor-
rection, for [a]instruction in righteousness, that the man of God
may be complete, thoroughly equipped for every good work."*

II Timothy 3:14-17

We are called to continue. Jesus said it this way,

*"If you abide in Me, and My words abide in you, you[a] will
ask what you desire, and it shall be done for you."*

John 15:7

Our walk with the Lord must be daily and consistent. Let me
ask you this, how many meals have you gone without since last
week? On the other hand, how many times have you been in the
presence of the Lord since last Sunday? His Word says,

"Oh, taste and see that the Lord is good;…"

Psalm 34:8

If we feed ourselves in the natural on an average of three times
a day, then how much more should we feed ourselves on the Word
of God? Jesus said,

*"…'Man shall not live by bread alone, but by every word that
proceeds from the mouth of God.'"*

Matthew 4:4

A mature relationship with God requires you to effectively manage your time with Him and His Word. There will never be maturation without the Word.

THE PLANTED SEED

"Let no one despise your youth, but be an example to the believers in word, in conduct, in love, in spirit, in faith, in purity. Till I come, give attention to reading, to exhortation, to doctrine. Do not neglect the gift that is in you, which was given to you by prophecy with the laying on of the hands of the eldership. Meditate on these things; give yourself entirely to them, that your progress may be evident to all. Take heed to yourself and to the doctrine. Continue in them, for in doing this you will save both yourself and those who hear you."

I Timothy 4:12-16

I got saved when I was 16 years, old as a junior in high school. At that time, God dropped *I Timothy 4:12-16* into my heart. As a teen, I recall my first encounter with a prophetic ministry. The visiting preacher started prophesying and said, "there's a young man here that God desires to use in the ministry through that of healing and to send throughout the world to share this gospel." I received that in my heart then and I am continuously seeing that manifest in my life. Prophetic words have been foundational and directional along my journey.

When the Word of God goes forth, you must wrap your faith

around it. You might say, "God, I don't know how You are going to do it.", "I don't know how You are going to make it happen.", or "God, I don't even know how You are going to work it out, but I am grabbing Your Word by faith." Being able to receive by faith is a must. Before you can receive a thing in the natural, you must first receive it in your heart by faith. It will never take place if you do not first believe it in your heart. There will be things that you believe in your heart, but you will not know how God is going to accomplish those things. All you can do is believe and know that He WILL do it! If you believe and receive it in your heart, then you can rest assured it shall manifest. Whatever is in your heart is coming out – it will come to pass.

In *I Timothy 4:15*, Paul instructs us not to neglect the gift within us and to meditate on all we have been taught. When you meditate, you are rehearsing a thing over and over. You are allowing it to stir up inside of you. Do not allow the Word to become dormant. It was over 40 years ago when I heard this proceeding Word of God for my life. This Word began to shape and mold me for my call, purpose, and destiny. He started maturing and developing me and I am where I am today because of His spoken Word many years ago. Yet, I still have not arrived. God has so much more for me and for all who have accepted Him as Lord and Savior and have adhered to His spoken Word for their lives. You may have received a Word from God and maybe it has not manifested, but now, it's birthing time! God is not a man that He should lie. If God said it, it will come to pass.

As you continue in the doctrine, not only will you save yourself, but you will save them that hear you. I decreed in my heart many years ago that I would be saved, as well as my whole family and I have seen that come to pass. Praise God! God is not finished yet; there is still room at the cross and I believe there are still family members and friends that will come. I encourage you to make a decree over your life, your family, and your friends just as I have done and watch God move.

CHAPTER 4

The Valley Gate

THE PLACE OF HUMILITY

"The Valley Gate was repaired by Hanun and the residents of Zanoah. They rebuilt it and put its doors with their bolts and bars in place."

Nehemiah 3:13

There will be seasons where it seems that everything you touch prospers, and then other seasons where you go through valleys. When you go through valleys, do not be afraid because even in the midst, God provides comfort, protection, and wisdom.

The Valley Gate is the place where lessons of humility are learned. There are some lessons that we can only learn during our valley experiences because in the Kingdom of God, the way up is sometimes down. Many people think that once they are saved, they will live on the mountaintop for the rest of their lives. However, part of our spiritual development by God will take place in the valley.

"Blessed is the man whose strength is in You, whose heart is set on pilgrimage. As they pass through the Valley of Baca, they make it a spring; The rain also covers it with pools. They go from strength to strength; Each one appears before God in Zion."

Psalm 84:5-7

Valleys are transitional places. As much as we love the high and lofty places of our lives, we rarely move from mountaintop to mountaintop. Most of the time, that pilgrimage requires you to go through the valley. David refers to the Valley of Baca, which is the valley of sorrow. This is not a beautiful, majestic, or desirable place; however, it is required terrain. Nor is it a place of punishment, it is a place of emotional and spiritual preparation. This is a place of pain. The Valley of Baca is not a dwelling place for you or a place of long-term residency. It is not a place for you to throw up a tent and camp out, rather a place you must press through.

This valley of sorrow is connected with great and profound grief and loss. The loss of a loved one that meant the world to you. The divorce, which dismantled every part of your being. The loss of trusted relationships through betrayal. The pain of no longer being accepted by those you have previously been in relationship with. Rejected and alienated from those that you have assisted, poured life into, and encouraged when they were going through their Valley of Baca experience. Those that you have graciously reached out to offering your support and encouragement, yet during your experience they do not have the decency to reach out with a simple word of encouragement. These are some examples of the Valley of Baca experiences that unfortunately we have or will experience.

There will be some devastating experiences that will happen in ministry, business, and in your personal life that will literally shake you to the core. However, as devastating and painful as it is, it will ultimately produce a weight of glory that nothing else would have been able to yield. Paul described it this way,

"We are hard-pressed on every side, yet not crushed; we are perplexed, but not in despair; persecuted, but not forsaken; struck down, but not destroyed;"

II Corinthians 4:8-9

Regretfully, we are losing and disengaging too many during this aspect of their journey. I realized this firsthand going through the separation and divorce of my 27-year marriage. Next to the death of my sister, Veronica, in 1995 to Sickle Cell and the sudden passing of my best friend and brother Kevin in 1997, I had never in my entire life experienced this depth of pain.

The level of personal unraveling my divorce produced was mind blowing. I literally hit some emotional low places that I did not know were possible. Simultaneously, I was dealing with the closure of the relationship with the church that I started in 1997. The current leadership felt that it was necessary for them to go in another direction that no longer needed my voice or engagement.

All of this was occurring while, for the first time in my life, I was functioning as a single father with both of my children living with me in an 1800 square foot condominium. My daughter Keira Iman was 23 years old and attending cosmetology school and my son Jordan, was 15 years old, and a high school freshman. Extremely layered and challenging emotionally, spiritually, and financially, this was a Valley of Baca that I was not equipped nor prepared for. The perfect storm; the tipping point.

I had to make some intentional decisions. My emotional and spiritual health took precedence over everything. For the first time in my life, self-care became my priority, something I had never considered before. I had always given my whole heart, energy, and strength to the churches that I served, with no thought of self-care. From my first pastorate at Bethany Baptist Church in Richmond, VA at the age of 23 during my last year of undergraduate at Virginia Union University, to leading Living Waters Christian Fellowship, a multi-million dollar non-denominational church, while also providing global oversight to ministries nationally and internationally.

Between those two pastoral tenures, I pastored Mt. Nebo Baptist Church in West Point, VA, which was considered one of the premier rural churches in America. Mt. Nebo was steeped in tradition and the singing of anthems. This was where some of the best-educated and most loving people were reared and rooted. From there, I pastored Colossian Baptist Church in Newport News, VA where we experienced over 300 individuals connecting to the church during the two years I served.

My introduction to Colossian Baptist was through Dr. Leonidas (Lee) Young Jr. During that time, he was the pastor of the Fourth Baptist Church in Richmond, VA and served as the Mayor of the city of Richmond. Personally, he was like a big brother to me. He was one of the rare individuals who always supported and offered invaluable counsel along my journey. We laughed and cried together. With the sudden passing of my brother, Lee would provide invaluable support and counsel to my family and me by eulogizing Kevin.

Within just a few short years, I found myself providing love and support to him as he was released from federal incarceration and was assigned to a halfway house in Newport News, VA where my ministry was based. Our ministry graciously loved and poured into his life during this Valley of Baca season. It was one of the most meaningful displays of ministry that I had witnessed and been a part of. There was no trace of judgment or abandonment shown to this man of God from my ministry or from me personally. We all felt that we were called to bring healing and hope to him as a servant of God. His case and exposure received national attention, yet this was my brother who changed the whole trajectory of my life and ministry.

One of the saddest days I have witnessed was on his sentencing day. The only other preacher in the courtroom that day that I recognized was Dr. Vander Warner, illustrious pastor of the Grove Avenue Baptist Church in Richmond, VA. Lee was one of the most intelligent minds I had ever encountered. His preaching ability opened doors for him across the nation. Not only was he a dear brother to me, but he was also a brother to so many others throughout America. Yet on this day, only a few stood with Lee on his darkest day. My heart broke for my brother and his family for the utter abandonment he experienced. I saw, firsthand, how Lee and his family sacrificially traveled throughout this country, blessing and encouraging others publicly and privately because of the grace and influence upon his life. Yet during his Valley of Baca experience, there was no reciprocity.

So many others have their own Valley of Baca experience, some private, some public, some known, and some unknown. My heart has always been to connect with the brokenhearted and to offer hope and support. I have done that for years, not only with Lee, but also with those who were engaged in my ministry and beyond. Through God's grace, I have provided emotional and financial support for families burying their babies, offered housing for those who had gone through bankruptcy or medical challenges, offered compassionate counseling for pastors dealing with marital issues, supported and established ministries from their inception, and introduced leaders to some of the most honored and recognized ministry leaders in the world. As much as possible, I used the platform and influence that God gave to me to support and to encourage others publicly and privately without any judgment or expectation of payback.

Going through my valley was devastating. I lost it all. Yet while hurting on so many fronts, I knew that I would endure and get through that season. My focus was solely asking God to heal not Apostle Banks or Bishop Banks but me, Steven the person. The grim reality was that others benefitted from Apostle or Bishop as long as they could. Yet during this low season, I was floored at how so many sons, ministerial friends, and covenant relationships did not have the basic Christian courtesy to reach out to offer a simple kind word such as, "I'm praying for you" or, "so sorry to hear" or, "wishing you the best."

Many of these were individuals and leaders throughout the country who would reach out to me in the heat of marital arguments to minister to them in moments that they wanted to walk away from ministry, from marriage, and some from life altogether. These were relationships that I not only opened my ministry to, but I opened my house to in order to offer them a safe and restful place in which to retreat and heal. There were individuals who valued my ministry, but did not have the finances to pay for my travel and lodging. I would then go into my personal account to secure airfare and hotel accommodations to travel to their church in order to pour into their church and ministerial families without receiving any honorarium at all. This happened so many times I cannot even recall. There were so many that had access to me, knowing that I was only a phone call away whenever they were going through their own valley experience or just desired a listening ear; I was literally amazed at how quickly they all scattered.

My ex-wife no longer wanted to be involved in ministry and wanted to pursue other ventures. I fully understood where she was with her journey. Ministry is and has been my life calling. In support of her desires, we relocated from Virginia to Atlanta to give ourselves an opportunity to start afresh, however that may have looked. Moving to Atlanta for me was much more about my family then my ministry. However, we began to recognize that we were on two significantly different paths, and after years of counseling and making adjustments we came to the decision that we were better off going our separate ways.

I never knew how my divorce would be the entrance to my experience of the Valley of Baca. David stated that while *"Passing through the Valley of Baca maketh it a well; the rain also filleth the pool."* With your tears and with the rains that life produces, you make it a well.

Your valley of sorrow becomes a well through your tears. Sometimes you will have to cry. Some life situations will bring suffering, tears, pain, and hardship. These types of situations are valley experiences that God allows you to go through. They will cause you many tears and much pain, but you will be able to return to your well for the refreshing presence of God. You will be able to look back on the ordeals that caused you to fill a well full of tears and give a testimony of praise because God brought you through! You will be able to testify that you would never have known the power of God like you know it now, had you not gone through your valley.

What you thought would devastate you, God will use as an avenue of elevation in your life.

"And we know that all things work together for good to those who love God, to those who are the called according to His purpose."

Romans 8:28

All things means ALL THINGS. Even the things we think are bad work for our good.

"...weeping may endure for a night but joy comes in the morning."

Psalm 30:5

"Those who sow in tears shall reap in joy. He who continually goes forth weeping, bearing seed for sowing, shall doubtless come again with rejoicing, bringing his sheaves with him."

Psalm 126:5-6

We will all experience painful seasons in our lives. There will be seasons of trials and hardship, but God says joy will come in the morning. We will all have valley experiences. In those times,

"...look up and lift up your heads, because your redemption draws near."

Luke 21:28

Just as the morning is the dawning of a new day and as the sun breaks through at sunrise, so too will your valley experience end with a breakthrough! Your morning will come after you have stood faithful through your night. When God sheds light over your situation, you can expect a new day and the beginning of a new season to be released over your life.

HUMILITY REQUIRES RELEASING

"Likewise you younger people, submit yourselves to your elders. Yes, all of you be submissive to one another, and be clothed with humility, for "God resists the proud, But gives grace to the

*humble." Therefore humble yourselves under the mighty hand
of God, that He may exalt you in due time, casting all your care
upon Him, for He cares for you."*

I Peter 5:5-7

I have found great strength from my Valley of Baca experience. Your trials have a way of manifesting God's glory and grace over your life in ways that you have never imagined. Baca teaches you to rely solely on God. Regardless of the details of your situation, you will find during this season that all you can do is release and humble yourself to the process. There will be layers of pride, resentment, and bitterness over people and circumstances in your life. However, humility requires you to deal with all the wounds of your broken heart so that God is able to heal you. Pride is derived from a false sense of entitlement. Humility is the avenue whereby God is allowed to enter the cold and dark places of your heart. The Word says,

"...God resists the proud, but gives grace to the humble."

James 4:6

THE SNARE OF THE DEVIL

"How you are fallen from heaven, O Lucifer, son of the morning! How you are cut down to the ground, You who weakened the nations! For you have said in your heart: I will ascend into heaven, I will exalt my throne above the stars of God; I will also sit on the mount of the congregation, On the farthest sides of the

north; I will ascend above the heights of the clouds, I will be like the Most High. Yet you shall be brought down to Sheol, To the lowest depths of the Pit."

Isaiah 14:12-15

Pride was the downfall of the enemy. It caused Lucifer, the son of the morning, to be rejected and evicted from the throne room of God. Pride is self-reliance and independence. Pride is not just relying on yourself, but pride says you can do it without God. God desires for us to be clothed with humility. Apostolic centers must maintain an atmosphere of humility. Humility is dependency upon God. We are not able to execute our assignments relying solely upon our own ability, nor will we be able to be delivered from our pain by ourselves.

In the above passage, notice how many times Lucifer says, "I will". He makes this declaration five times! He says, "**I will** ascend into heaven." Then he says, "**I will** exalt my throne upon the stars of God." Again he says, "**I will** sit upon the mount in the congregation in the side of the north." He then says, "**I will** ascend upon the height of the clouds." Finally, he says, "**I will** be like the most High God." This is quite literally self-exaltation! We learn from the Word that God resists the proud. The same snares that caused the enemy's downfall can also cause ours. Pride, an independent spirit, and thinking more highly of ourselves than of God will bring us down. The result of pride is found in Isaiah,

"Yet you shall be brought down to Sheol, To the lowest depths of the Pit."

Isaiah 14:15

Understand that God is not looking for you to make your name great or for you to exalt yourself, but He is looking for a willing and obedient heart. In our brokenness, we truly experience the healing power of God. As we connect to those who are going through painful and shameful situations in their lives, we truly represent His heart.

"And whoever exalts himself will be humbled, and he who humbles himself will be exalted."

Matthew 23:12

The Word of God says to "humble yourselves" and in due time He will exalt you. There are three vital points in this scripture: *First*, you are to humble yourself. In the midst of your valley is the perfect time to self-reflect and sincerely ask and trust the Lord to show you yourself. Humility does not seek to find blame or fault in others, but it opens our hearts to ask God to teach us the lessons we need to learn from the experiences. *Second*, there is a due time for those who are humbled that the enemy cannot hinder, block, or prevent. There is an expiration time where your suffering will no longer have a stronghold upon your life. God will now be able to use that suffering as a testimony of how He healed and delivered you from the pain connected. As you endure hardships and wait patiently, you are going to see the manifestation of God's glory over that which tried to destroy you. *Third*, He will exalt you. As you are open to the healing of God, He will exalt you so that you will testify of His goodness in and through your life. Shame and failure will be removed from your life because your focus will be solely upon how the Lord made His presence known to you in your lonely and abandoned state. He seals His covenant with you while you are at the Valley Gate. Elevation takes place at the Valley Gate as we posture our hearts to trust God completely throughout the process.

The building of the tower of Babel in *Genesis 11* is a perfect example of what can happen when we become prideful and try to take matters into our own hands. In verse four of that chapter, when the people said, "...*let us make a tower...*" they were really saying let us make a name for ourselves. Anytime you try to lift yourself up on your own, you are in trouble. You were not created to live outside of the will of God. When you think you can do a thing outside of the will of God and think that you do not need Him, you may have success for a season, but it is not going to la~~. You need to make sure that God is in the midst of any sit~ ~on in your life.

"And He said to me, "My grace is sufficie~ore, most gladly I strength is made perfect in weaknes~the power of Christ may will rather boast in my infirmi~re in infirmities, in re- rest upon me. Therefore, I~ in distresses, for Christ's sake. proaches, in needs, in ~m strong."
For when I am ~

II Corinthians 12:9–10

WHY THE VALLEY?

Know that your valley experiences are not to humiliate you; rather they are opportunities for personal growth and development in the midst of crisis. Even though discouragement comes with these experiences, they yield great encouragement as you navigate these painful ordeals. They are not designed to kill you, but to strengthen you. God wants to show you His strength and His power. At the Valley Gate is where you recognize that His grace is more than sufficient to carry you through things you thought you could not handle. Some people will wonder how you will make it through. They know about your estranged husband. They know about your pregnant teenage daughter. They know about the son that is in and out of court. They know about your addiction. They know that you have filed for bankruptcy. They know about your home going into foreclosure and your vehicle being repossessed. They know about the doctor's terminal report. Yet and still, they see you with a smile on your face and praise in your heart. Why? How? It is so because you know that His grace is sufficient! It is in our weakness that we truly experience His strength. It is where His strength is made perfect in weakness. There are some things that you will know beyond through because once you come out, you will know who brought you out! You will know beyond the shadow of doubt that it was Him who brought you out! Only the Lord could have that only God can get the glory! Only the Lord could have me through the dark-est season of my life. Psalm 84 says

"They go from strength to strength"

96

Psalm 84:7

Even in your low times personally, professionally, or ministerially, continually remind yourself that God's strength is sufficient. Share that with others who have come to a Valley of Baca experience. People need your encouraging presence, not your judgment or abandonment.

With very few trusted and encouraging voices to provide their comforting presence, I relied solely upon His strength, because there were days I just did not want to get out of bed. Yet through it all, I knew that God would bring me to the other side. I vividly remember His Spirit speaking to me to let me know that "my suffering had redemptive value". I knew in my heart that I was going to get through it. As my focus was upon my self-care, I also know that I had to navigate Iman and Jordan wisely and safely through this as well. As painful as this situation was, I really sensed that their presence brought collective healing to us. Going from a 7,500 square foot, 8-bedroom house with a pool overlooking the 13th hole on one of the most prestigious golf courses in the area, to a 1,800 square foot condominium was a major adjustment. However, this valley, in the most painful season of my life and my ministry, turned out to be the most rewarding chapter in my life.

When you bring God into your valley situation, you recognize that you must lean on and totally trust Him to work it out. You no longer care or worry about what will happen; you cast your cares upon Him because you know that He cares for you. There will be some storms and some adversities in your life, but the fact is, when you turn it over to Jesus, you know that you are coming out victorious, you are coming out with a praise, and you are coming out with favor because you have put your trust in Him.

KINGDOM EXALTATION

Kingdom operation is the opposite of the worldly system. If you lift yourself up in the Kingdom of God, you will fall. On the other hand, as you humble yourself in the Kingdom, you shall be raised or lifted to higher heights. So then, one of the principles or keys to kingdom operations is if you want to go up in the Kingdom of God, you have to go down.

"He must increase, but I must decrease."

John 3:30

The Kingdom of God is an upside-down kingdom, and it operates completely different from the order or the mindset that we have been taught. If you want to receive in the Kingdom, you must give. If you want to go up in the Kingdom, you have to go down. In the world, to be viewed as great means you have acquired wealth, stature, and a name for yourself. And in obtaining your wealth, stature, and name, quite often you have treated people any kind of way, but God says not so in the Kingdom.

God is seeking those who are willing to walk in humility. The Bible tells us,

"...God resists the proud, But gives grace to the humble." Therefore humble yourselves under the mighty hand of God,..."

I Peter 5:5-6

It is at the Valley Gate where God allows humility to be developed and matured.

"Pride goes before destruction and a haughty spirit before a fall."

Proverbs 16:18

Wherever there is pride, destruction will follow. A haughty spirit will always come before a fall. A haughty spirit is a spirit of arrogance. It is a contemptuous spirit that is blatantly disrespectful. In our judicial system, we hear of individuals being held in contempt. That means they have blatantly been disrespectful to the order, to the procedure, or to the operation of the court or the judge. Individuals held in contempt can be fined or can even go to jail. If that is how contempt is looked upon in the legal system, how much more unacceptable is it in the Kingdom of God?

It is solely by the grace of God that you are where you are today. It is not because of who you know or do not know. It is not because of what you have done or what you have accomplished, but it is solely by His grace. Whenever we frustrate the grace of God, we no longer walk in His favor or under an open heaven. When we take His grace for granted, God will take His grace from you and give it to someone else.

Your valley of sorrow becomes a well through your tears. Pain happens in ministry. Pain happens in life. Pain happens in business. We all experience seasons like this. Apostolic centers create healthy spaces and provide support through modeling connections, building covenant relationships, and providing compassion when individuals find themselves in their Valley of Baca. It is here that authentic and meaningful relationships show up for you and not scatter from you.

CHAPTER 5

The Dung Gate
THE PLACE OF CLEANSING

"The Dung Gate was repaired by Malkijah son of Rekab, ruler of the district of Beth Hakkerem. He rebuilt it and put its doors with their bolts and bars in place."

Nehemiah 3:14 NIV

The Dung Gate symbolizes cleansing. The Dung Gate was utilized for sanitation purposes. It was the gate used to discard, release, and eliminate trash from the city. It was their waste management system. In our application, the Dung Gate deals with the removal of matters that will stain us inwardly. Inner cleansing from issues that will pollute your heart, as well as the atmosphere. The city remained sanitized as waste and trash was removed consistently. Likewise, we are cleansed inwardly as we address and deal with matters of the heart so they will not fester and negatively affect our heart and atmosphere.

"...You desire truth in the inward parts,..."

Psalm 51:6

"Keep your heart with all diligence, For out of it spring the issues of life."

Proverbs 4:23

Matters of the heart such as bitterness, jealousy, anger, and unforgiveness left undealt with, will slowly cause decay within our souls. When food begins to spoil, it is rarely noticeable as long as the refrigerator remains closed. However, the more the door opens, the more noticeable the decay becomes. Just as spoiled food needs to be disposed of, our confession serves to remove the decay of our heart and thoughts. Our mouths also serve as an indicator to let us know the conditions of our heart.

"If we confess our sins, he is faithful and just and will forgive us our sins..."

I John 1:9

Every apostolic center must have a Dung Gate that operates properly so that two things take place: waste is released, and anything that would promote an unhealthy environment is addressed. We must make sure that the atmosphere within apostolic centers is not toxic. Without the Dung Gate, you will have a toxic environment filled with a stench that will block the sweet aroma of the presence of God. Any atmosphere that fails to address heart matters, over time, will become unhealthy. Oftentimes healthy lines of communication are not established, resulting in individuals holding matters within. This happens in relationships, businesses, and ministries. When this undercurrent occurs, the anointing is compromised and contamination becomes possible.

The Dung Gate was used for waste management. A city without a Dung Gate will be polluted and affect your health. God created the human body with a natural means of excreting waste.

He created an avenue for release, not only in the physical body, but also in the body of Christ. Just as an individual can be constipated, a church can be constipated and bloated. It is very possible to mistake swelling for growth. A compromised atmosphere will affect your development and your spiritual maturity.

CONFESSION

As we look at the meaning of the words Dung Gate in the Hebrew language, it literally means confession. As we confess, we release the sins and wrong doings from our lives. Through our confession, we are healed; we are cleansed. In the spirit realm, it is at the Dung Gate that God brings healing to us personally and to our atmosphere.

The Dung Gate cleanses and renews unhealthy environments. This is not an occasional activity; it must be systematic and occur regularly. It takes more than a singular action, an atmosphere must be consciously created and continually cultivated.

"Make every effort to live in peace with everyone and to be holy; without holiness no one will see the Lord. See to it that no one falls short of the grace of God and that no bitter root grows up to

cause trouble and defile many."

Hebrews 12:14-15 NIV

"Get rid of all bitterness, rage and anger, brawling and slander, along with every form of malice. Be kind and compassionate to one another, forgiving each other, just as in Christ God forgave you."

Ephesians 4:31-32 NIV

As a believer, chaos and confusion should not be a part of your character. Ideally, there should be no animosity, resentment, hostility, and offense in the atmosphere. Confessing heals our hearts and our atmosphere.

I recall a time when I was resigning from a former pastorate. Things were chaotic and confusion was abounding as I shared in an earlier chapter. The environment was unhealthy and not conducive for my leadership style. The Spirit of the Lord spoke to my spirit one Thursday night as soon as I sat down at the table for a joint board meeting. The joint board consisted of individuals who served as deacons and trustees of this church. Without any prior consideration or thoughts, as soon as I sat down, the Holy Spirit spoke to me and said, *"I'm releasing you to the Body"*. From that night on, I began to share privately with a few individuals, who were specifically connected to me and to my assignment. In fact, all of these individuals had shared with me privately over prior months that they were hoping and praying for me to start a church.

At no time in my life, up to that moment, had I ever considered starting a church. I had never seen that before in my journey and those who I had heard of that started churches were individuals who had storefront churches and had not experienced major growth. Additionally, embedded in the back of my mind was the prophetic word that I heard as a teenager calling me to nations. Nevertheless, six weeks later I was starting Living Waters Christian Fellowship, with the support of about ten people who worked behind the scenes making it happen.

In most churches, the pastor's notice of resignation is given anywhere from two to four weeks prior to them leaving. Due to the tense environment, my planning team thought that it would be best and safest if my possessions were moved out of my office late Saturday night, since my resignation the next day would be effective immediately. The atmosphere was fraught. Physical and verbal threats were being made. That particular Sunday was Communion Sunday. My intentions were to simply share a brief sermon, announce my resignation and vacate the premises. We had an evening service scheduled that day as well. Our guest was a nationally known Evangelist whom I had shared my plans with prior to her arrival. I wanted her to be able to have the opportunity to withdraw or to decline the invitation based on the atmosphere and transition that was about to take place.

She gave me some of the wisest counsel that I heard during that time. As a friend and a five-fold leader she shared with me that communion was not about me or about what was taking place. The communion was solely about what Jesus has done for us all. She reminded me that what I was going through was larger than me, or anything that had happened in the relationship with that church. This was a Kingdom move.

She strongly encouraged me that, as the pastor, I should still serve communion and be faithful to my pastoral service. Adhering to her counsel, I served communion to each deacon and publicly decreed over each one "the blessings of the Lord be upon you". As I shared and served each one, speaking blessings over them, including those who were involved in creating the chaos, my healing began to take place. This process of healing took some time but, fortunately, it did happen. Many of those individuals connected to that church have followed my ministry over the years, and we now share a great and mutual respect.

DO NOT EAT OF THE BITTER FRUIT

There is always a root cause to any symptom or problem we encounter. For complete healing to be manifested, the issue must be attacked at the root. The root is simply its origin, its basic core, or its beginning. You cannot see a root. You can see the fruit, but not the root. Unless we deal with the root of bitterness, there may be things in our heart that defile us, however, this root has not been given the opportunity to manifest yet. Some things may have simply been repressed or avoided. These issues will eventually leak out in actions, thoughts, or words.

An apostolic center must be a healthy environment where individuals can share their thoughts and feelings. Any healthy environment must have open and honest conversations. Individuals need a process that grants them opportunities to share from their hearts without any retribution or isolation. For too long the only conversations that pastors hear about are disclosed after disgruntled members have left the ministry. Avoidance is never the healthy answer. Going to another church is not resolving the inner matters. Healing is required, whether a person leaves or stays. Unfortunately, few churches are healthy enough to hear and to make suggested changes. If the leadership is fragile themselves, they will shut down communication in every possible way, including monitoring and controlling your social media platform. In toxic environments, communication is always one-sided.

That is extremely dangerous on so many levels. The openness of communication is a great indicator of the health of any relationship. It may not be necessary or even appropriate for everyone to speak directly to the leader, but there should be leaders within the organization for individuals to share their thoughts and heart concerning various matters. Especially when things have taken place that had a negative emotional or spiritual impact. Talking and confessing has a healing effect. It is when people are prohibited from sharing that they begin internalizing matters and that fosters an atmosphere where bitterness and offenses can and will take root.

Wise leadership will intentionally communicate effectively and will graciously deal with matters of misunderstanding. Not every misunderstanding should lead to separating from churches and severing relationships. Misunderstandings are a part of every relationship. Conflict will take place. Wise leadership understands this and utilizes the Dung Gate so that bitterness and offense do not contaminate the atmosphere.

We are given the pattern of addressing offenses from the Word of God. Far too many times, we quote scriptures verbatim, yet we lack so much understanding of the implication of those very scriptures. Every relationship, whether marital, sibling, business, or friendship, will have times of misunderstanding. Offenses will occur. If we feel that the parties involved in the relationship are loving and have our best interest at heart, then we must have opportunities to share when there is a disconnect or an offense. Whether harm is intended or not, people's feelings and thoughts matter. If someone is in a relationship and does not sense in their heart that their leadership genuinely cares for them, it is extremely difficult to receive from that leadership. You only can receive from those you truly honor, as well as those who honor you; all parties must reciprocate honor. When honor is violated, the transgression must be discussed so that the relationship is not breached. These are times that the Dung Gate must be accessed. That requires open and honored lines of communication.

Typically, where there is an offense, it is always best for individuals to discuss and to work it out amongst themselves. Remember, the aim is to restore and to safeguard the relationship. It will require courageous conversations. For example, over the years members from various churches and in various situations have contacted me, sharing particular matters regarding their leaders that have offended them. My response has always been "you must talk to your leaders or to your leadership team to share your heart on that matter." Too often, they have never shared with their leaders what they were now sharing with me.

What is concerning is when individuals do not sense in their hearts that leadership really has their best interest at heart. So often, that can be much larger than an individual issue, but points to a systemic dysfunction. Leaders, for various reasons, may have greatly reduced and restricted lines of communication due to their insecurity and/or thinking that their authority is being "questioned". How many leaders have opened their hearts and been betrayed or damaged by the very ones they endeavor to lead? Regardless, we must access the Dung Gate if we desire to have fully engaged and activated individuals involved within our organizations.

"If a fellow believer hurts you, go and tell him. Work it out between the two of you. If he listens, you've made a friend. If he won't listen, take one or two others along so that the presence of witnesses will keep things honest, and try again. If he still won't listen, tell the church. If he won't listen to the church, you'll have to start over from scratch, confront him with the need for repentance, and offer again God's forgiving love."
Matthew 18:15-17 MSG

The word bitterness comes from the root word bitter, which means sharp or biting to the taste. Bitterness is harbored hurt. Bitterness blocks the flow of God's blessings in your life. Bitterness desires to take root in your heart and grow to produce hatred, jealousy, envy, and depression. Not only will bitterness affect your heart, hindering you from a free-flowing relationship with God, but it will abort your life's destiny.

Bitterness is like the bite of a poisonous snake. When a snake bites, it releases venom, and the poison enters your body and heads straight into the bloodstream. It is a direct hit to the blood because the enemy knows better than anyone that the power is in the blood. It is a direct bite or shot by the enemy precisely aimed to poison your heart. If you do not guard your heart from the fiery darts of the enemy, bitterness will hit you so suddenly that you will not even know you have been hit. It can become just as destructive as a blood clot.

There may come a time when someone will say or do something that may hurt or bother you and, in that moment, you may say to yourself, "What they did or said didn't really bother me, I forgive them." Somehow, over time, you begin to think about the situation and what was said. It will not be long before you find yourself upset at everyone and everything for no apparent reason. You have been bitten. The fact is you have a root of bitterness.

Bitterness is harboring past hurts. Holding on to the hurts of your past can poison your present and your future. Continuously experiencing pain without addressing it over time will create walls that become a defense mechanism. All your pains and wounds left undealt with are hoarded behind that wall. Since they have no outlet, they are held captive within. Eventually, your heart hardens. When you release these pains, you open the door to your liberty. After all, harboring unforgiveness and bitterness is not holding the offender hostage; rather it is holding you hostage.

During my time of self-care, this was one of the most challenging parts of the healing journey. The deep feeling of abandonment produced a profound sense of bitterness. How could those that I have invested in over the years, without reservation, withdraw totally as if I were accursed. The level of abandonment was beyond anything that I could have imagined. I definitely understood their pain and hurt over my divorce, but no one on the outside hurt more than I did. I would have been more understanding if my divorce placed them in a posture of shame or disgrace due to public embarrassment or scandal. That was not the case at all. To experience total isolation from those that I personally counseled during their hardships was disheartening. These individuals that shared life and ministry with me. Nevertheless, I was reminded by Holy Spirit that I could not allow this to fester. Healing required me to feel that abandonment in order to process my pain. This was a continuous inner work. I was determined not to allow my bitterness to hinder the healing for which I longed.

THE COVENANT

Due to the root of bitterness that is prevalent in so many lives, people choose not to enter into covenant. Because of past hurts, many are reluctant to share their feelings fully, especially in the area of their pain. The greater the relationship or covenant, the greater the pain. That is why the termination of the marital covenant is so layered and so painful to bring closure to. No one has shared more of your life, joys, and pain than your former spouse has. They know what makes you happy and what makes you sad. They have the ability to touch nerves that you never even knew existed in your life. Because of the depth of intimacy that has occurred within the marriage, it is important that proper recovery time be given due to the depth of the relationship. Even in the case of short-term relationships, it is important that the time and focus of healing be properly attended to as well. The length of the relationship is a factor, but just as pivotal is the amount of hope, dreams, energy, and passion that one placed upon the relationship.

It is not easy to walk away from a covenant relationship that has been broken. This is common with people who have been hurt while serving under another ministry. They move on, but are harboring hurt from their prior experience, so they are unwilling to trust anyone. The fact is, they may be physically present in another congregation, but they have not entered a covenant with their current shepherd due to their woundedness. There is a root of bitterness or offense in their heart that is based on a prior relationship. They are hindered in their present and future relationships based on the hurts of their past. Therefore, the current relationship is unable to receive their full engagement due to past experiences.

GRIEVING

"And do not grieve the Holy Spirit of God [do not offend or vex or sadden Him], by whom you were sealed (marked, branded as God's own, secured) for the day of redemption (of final deliv-

erance through Christ from evil and the consequences of sin).
Let all bitterness and indignation and wrath (passion, rage,
bad temper) and resentment (anger, animosity) and quarrel-
ing (brawling, clamor, contention) and slander (evil-speaking,
abusive or blasphemous language) be banished from you, with
all malice (spite, ill will, or baseness of any kind). And be-
come useful and helpful and kind to one another, tenderhearted
(compassionate, understanding, loving-hearted), forgiving one
another [readily and freely], as God in Christ forgave you."
Ephesians 4:30-32 AMP

We all know the pain associated with grief. Every loss needs
space to grieve, whether the loss of a loved one, a job, a relationship, or health condition. Grief is never easy and has its various
stages. When grieving, it is as if you are in a fog or haze. Time
seems to be slowing down. One feels totally disconnected and
lost. As painful as that is for us, Paul shares that the Holy Spirit
grieves as we allow bitterness, rage, unforgiveness, anger, and slander to go unchecked in our lives. This saddens God's Spirit and
should cause us grief as well.

We know the hurt that we experience when we have been
offended. Such is the case with God's Spirit. He is grieved when
we have bitterness, envy, resentment, and malice within our hearts.
apostolic centers must create atmospheres that will be conducive
for healing and encourage forgiveness to be released.

The Dung Gate must be in full operation to keep the environment healthy and pure. These environments are places that do not
allow bitterness and resentment to dwell there. These are loving

and forgiving houses, where judgment is not in the atmosphere. Judgment has been removed from the equation because individuals have experienced the healing and forgiving power of the Lord during their time of offense, pain, and bitterness.

The gracious and sovereign work of the Holy Spirit is what brings healing in our lives at the deepest place of pain that we have endured. That is inner healing. This healing is available when you intentionally yield to His working within your life. My heart goes out to pastors, spouses, and other visible leaders who have gone through or are currently going through divorce, separation, death, or any other significant loss. Healing is difficult enough privately, it is infinitely more complicated and extremely challenging when a leader goes through this publicly while still pastoring or trying to lead with a vision.

MENTAL HEALTH

Apostolic centers must take the lead in modeling mental and emotional health as well.

"Beloved, I pray that you may prosper in all things and be in health, just as your soul prospers."

III John 2

Apostolic centers will draw individuals who have an extraordinarily strong anointing, gifting, and personality, and rarely lend themselves to people with passive personalities. There is a genetic wiring for "apostolic people", therefore leaders must be secure and healthy not only spiritually, but also emotionally and mentally. Insecure leaders will revert to control and manipulation to get people to follow them. When other strong, creative, and skilled leaders connect with their vision, it will not intimidate healthy leaders. Emotionally driven leaders create a deep sense of uncertainty within ministry. Narcissistic leaders are very insecure and will place a heavy and often unrealistic burden upon leadership. The more that narcissistic leaders can control your time and movement, the less time you have to realize how unhealthy the environment is because you are constantly busy with church work or with whatever makes their vision shine.

Those serving in leadership need to model wholeness, not perfection, to those they serve. The reality is that all of us need healing in our souls. That is where pain resides. Rejection, failure, shame, bitterness, PTSD, and abandonment are soul wounds. Left unaddressed, they fester and can contaminate an individual and every environment that they encounter. This is why Paul admonishes believers to work out the salvation (healing, health, and wholeness) of our souls. Left unchecked,

"Whoever has no rule over his own spirit is like a city broken down, without walls."

Proverbs 25:28

Stress levels increase considerably while carrying the daily and weekly demands of providing leadership. During the time of my separation and divorce, I intentionally focused on my mental and emotional health. My health and wholeness far outweighed my need to do ministry. Ministry must never become an addiction. Reducing my ministry assignment and load was a deliberate decision. I only accepted ministerial engagements that I had a full peace and release in my heart to serve. These engagements were not heavy warfare assignments, but places where I could provide encouragement as well as places that brought great encouragement and energy to my life without a "questioning" or "judgmental" environment.

LET GO AND LET GOD

The implication of the Dung Gate is that your past hurts, offenses, and disappointments are released, and you are cleansed and purged. Now you are an opened vessel available for use by God. The cleansing and refreshing presence of God begins to permeate the atmosphere. It is no longer an atmosphere of condemnation and shame, but one of forgiveness, refreshment, and restoration. Healthy organizations do not have many undercurrents because they model and support authentic conversations.

Where have the miracles gone? Why aren't blessings freely flowing? Maybe we have allowed offense to go unaddressed. Maybe we have not created healthy and productive channels of communication for those we say that we are in relationships with. Maybe we have shouted and danced over the trauma that is now demanding our attention, so that we can deal with it and move past it. Maybe we have focused more on having titles than having sound minds. We must shift the narrative from unilateral to collaborative, pastoral to apostolic, from one to the many with meaningful dialogue that will empower every person to feel, share, and heal.

"For if you forgive other people when they sin against you, your heavenly Father will also forgive you. But if you do not forgive others their sins, your Father will not forgive your sins."

Matthew 6:14-15 NIV

There can be no unforgiveness, malice, bitterness, or anger in the presence of the Lord. When you learn to let it go, God will be able to do a work for you to mature you, to develop you and to increase your measure, but if you hang on to that bitterness, resentment, or anger, it will hinder your individual spiritual growth and frustrate the move of God. Forgiveness becomes the healing balm for your soul.

"And when you stand praying, if you hold anything against anyone, forgive them, so that your Father in heaven may forgive you your sins."

Mark 11:25 NIV

CHAPTER 6

The Fountain Gate

THE PLACE OF PROPHETIC ENGAGEMENT

"The Fountain Gate was repaired by Shallun son of Kol-Hozeh, ruler of the district of Mizpah. He rebuilt it, roofing it over and putting its doors and bolts and bars in place..."

Nehemiah 3:15

The Fountain Gate was the primary entrance to the springs that allowed the water to be released in Jerusalem. It was the major source of the city's irrigation system. What is most notable about the Fountain Gate is that of all the gates, it was the gate found to be in the most ruin. Some believe that this gate was the center of the attack during the siege of Jerusalem by the Babylonian Army. Likewise, in the spirit realm, the Fountain Gate, which is symbolic of prophetic streams, is the target of the concentrated satanic attack; the central focus of the enemy's attack.

The Fountain Gate is a place of refreshment. Every organization needs a Fountain Gate springing forth with the prophetic release that refreshes the atmosphere and replenishes those who serve. Anything that is stagnant or stifled must be challenged, confronted, and changed immediately. There is a need for a constant flow of the Holy Spirit. This is the essence of apostolic centers. The power of His Spirit! God is always cultivating, rousing, and refreshing His people and their assignments.

A fountain is a spring or source of water, the source or head of a stream. Water springs forth with lots of bubbling activity from a fountain. Similarly, the Spirit of God springs forth in His fullness at the Fountain Gate. The Fountain Gate speaks of the prophetic dimension that should be operative in apostolic centers on a continual basis. The power of God is released through the ministry of the Holy Spirit. This is a place of continuous outpouring, therefore we understand why it is always under severe attack and constant bombardment by the enemy.

BROKEN CISTERNS

"Has a nation changed its gods, Which are not gods? But My people have changed their Glory For what does not profit."
Jeremiah 2:11

"For My people have committed two evils: They have forsaken Me, the fountain of living waters, And hewn themselves cisterns—broken cisterns that can hold no water."
Jeremiah 2:13

Jeremiah said the people had changed their gods and they had exchanged their glory with something that does not profit them. They had changed to gods that were not producing or demonstrating results. He says they had committed two evils. On one hand, they had forsaken the fountain of living water and secondly, they had hewn their own cisterns that were broken and could not hold water. By forsaking the living water, they had restricted and reduced the continuous outpouring of the presence of God. They had abandoned the relationship with God and refused to communicate with Him. Instead of having fellowship with the Living Spring, they had turned towards the broken and self-made cistern's systems.

Cisterns are receptacles for holding water. In order for a cistern to be filled and stored for future use, the water itself must be brought in from another source. If a cistern is broken and cannot hold water, how can it hold joy and peace or anything else that the Lord will release to it? Hewing a cistern refers to a traditional mindset, system, or way of doing things. This way of thinking restricts God, because you expect Him to do what you ask and then do it your way, thus constraining His will and mobility. You will just have history when you can look back at what you have done or accomplished, because you have had no connection with the moving power of God that the spring of the living waters is producing. History is for us to draw strength from and to celebrate the works of God in our past, yet He uses history as a launching pad to let us know that He shall do greater as we attend to what He is currently saying.

A vital part of prophetic ministry is for the edification and exhortation of the people resulting in them being comforted. Even the people of God can and will become weary, but God is restoring and refilling them with the spirit of living waters.

"There is a river whose streams shall make glad the city of God, The holy place of the tabernacle of the Most High."

Psalm 46:4

"Now the Angel of the Lord found her by a spring of water in the wilderness, by the spring on the way to Shur."

Genesis 16:7

The angel of the Lord found Hagar near a fountain in the wilderness. While there with her son Ishmael, the angel of the Lord heard the child's cry and spoke from heaven. He led her to a well of water to be refreshed (*Gen 21:19*). We all go through wilderness experiences. That is why the Fountain Gate is so refreshing and needed by all at various times.

The Fountain Gate is a place where the Holy Spirit brings comfort to the afflicted. To those who have become weary and depleted along their journey. Doing life under the heavy hands of oppression and discouragement whether personally, racially, politically, socially, and/or economically, is draining. Single parents doing the absolute best they can to raise their children, because the other parent chooses not to be engaged in the raising of the child. Couples, who are now taking care of aging parents, all while taking care of their own children. Grandmothers, sacrificing their lives to raise grandchildren because the parents are incarcerated or deceased. Children caught up in the school-to-prison pipeline. Individuals who are in bondage to heroin/opioids. Those who are dealing with trauma who have no one to turn to or no insurance to receive mental and emotion help. It is at the Fountain Gate where comfort and encouragement are released to those who have been afflicted.

SOCIAL JUSTICE

> *"The Spirit of the Lord is upon Me, Because He has anointed Me To preach the gospel to the poor; He has sent Me to heal the brokenhearted, To proclaim liberty to the captives And recovery of sight to the blind, To set at liberty those who are oppressed. To proclaim the acceptable year of the Lord."*
>
> *Luke 4:18-19*

The prophetic word not only comforts the afflicted, it afflicts the comforted. Prophetic ministry is to "cry loud and spare not". It speaks to the establishment by addressing systemic injustice. Jesus, as the Great Liberator, addresses social injustice as a part of His Kingdom assignment. Racism perpetuates white privilege and supremacy. It is the dominate stronghold that has been perpetuated in American culture from its inception with its origins stemming from and supported by the church. It is idolatry in its purest form.

Prophetic ministry utters the voice of justice and liberation to oppressive systems and mindsets. Apostolic centers are catalysts for freedom and equality. As we are witnessing the racial upheaval sparked by the vicious murder of George Floyd by four police officers. Racial tensions are at an all-time high, not just in America, but globally. Brown and Black people are systemically marginalized and not given the same opportunities afforded to those of the establishment. People of color are dealing with the pipeline to prison, unemployment, underemployment, lack of health care, educational bias, higher incarceration rates, and so many other social issues that continue to cripple their overall advancement. The incarceration rate is highest for people of color. Long-standing systemic health and social inequities have put many people from racial and ethnic minority groups at increased risk of getting sick and dying from COVID-19. This virus has drastically affected people of color at a disproportionate rate.

Also affecting the minority community is the challenge of immigration reform. According to NBCnews.com, the U.S. held a record 69,550 migrant children in government custody in 2019 alone. While we address the current issues surrounding injustice and race, the lack of the presence of the evangelical church has been unbelievable and extremely disheartening to African Americans, especially to those who have supported these ministries as members and financial partners for years. The evangelical church has remained silent during these times. Dr. Martin Luther King was so accurate when he stated, "In the end, we will remember not the words of our enemies, but the silence of our friends".

I fully embrace and endorse multi-racial congregations where there is a complete level and celebration of diversity. Worship ought to integrate the various expressions of the diverse congregants as opposed to pulling everyone into the worship style of the dominate culture. Leadership ought to be reflective of those who are a part of the ministry, both in terms of race and gender. Too often in multi-racial congregations, individuals are expected to leave their uniqueness and diversity at the door in order to blend into the culture of the church, which in most cases are white evangelical conservatives. When, in fact, multi-cultural churches have a unique opportunity to model oneness through diversity as opposed to engulfing the mixture of races to accept "whiteness" as synonymous with Christianity. Healthy churches can appreciate and utilize diversity as a strength. For white led ministries to say that Black Lives Matter ought not be a political statement! A truly prophetic declaration would value the sanctity and equality of a people systemically oppressed for over 400 years.

Equally, there is a prophetic swelling taking place in addressing the demonization of patriarchy. Once again, the "church" is one of the last institutions to confront the subjugation and oppression of women. We have now elected, for the first time in history, a woman to the second highest office in America. Vice President Kamala Harris is the first person of African American and Asian American heritage to hold this position. As we see women entering prominent leadership positions previously held by men only, I am encouraged and excited about the insights and skills that these women will use to move our nation, our cities, and our organizations forward. Prophetically, it has always been the heart of God to bless, and both "male and female" should be used in serving humanity for His glory.

I remain baffled by the sight of churches and denominations consisting of 75-90% of women congregants, yet their leadership numbers fail to reflect this. How is it that an all-male fraternity can model a prophetic cry for justice and equality, when it is not operating justly concerning women and their equality? Apostolic centers are called to address racial and gender inequalities. Our prophetic witness is greatly weakened when we cry for justice, yet continue to perpetuate toxic masculinity denying women the same level of authority and privilege solely based on gender. These misogynistic practices are antiquated and not reflective of God's heart for His Kingdom. These practices will go unchecked if patriarchal masculinity is not confronted. This perversion only benefits and serves the fragmented egos and passions of wounded men. The Church of God is not an elite fraternity, nor is it a "good ole boy" network; rather it must be a leading prophetic agency addressing injustice that affects all of God's creation. It is the height of hypocrisy for us to cry out for racial justice, but remain blatantly silent on gender equality.

Below are just a few biblical references that address racial and gender discrimination:

"There is neither Jew nor Greek, there is neither slave nor free, there is neither male nor female; for you are all one in Christ Jesus."

Galatians 3:28

"Where there is neither Greek nor Jew, circumcised nor uncircumcised, barbarian, Scythian, slave nor free, but Christ is all and in all."

Colossians 3:11

"And it shall come to pass afterward That I will pour out My Spirit on all flesh; Your sons and your daughters shall prophesy, Your old men shall dream dreams, My menservants and on My maidservants I will pour out My Spirit in those days."

Joel 2:28-29

"For He Himself is our peace, who has made both one, and has broken down the middle wall of separation,"

Ephesians 2:14

"For by one Spirit we were all baptized into one body— whether Jews or Greeks, whether slaves or free—and have all been made to drink into one Spirit."

I Corinthians 12:13

"But if you show partiality, you commit sin, and are convicted by the law as transgressors."

James 2:9

"The stranger who dwells among you shall be to you as one born among you, and you shall love him as yourself; for you were strangers in the land of Egypt..."

Leviticus 19:34

"Therefore, whatever you want men to do to you, do also to them, for this is the Law and the Prophets."

Matthew 7:12

"... 'You shall love your neighbor as yourself.'"

Matthew 22:39

"... 'You know how unlawful it is for a Jewish man to keep company with or go to one of another nation. But God has shown me that I should not call any man common or unclean.'"

Acts 10:28

The legal and racial inequities are just as pronounced in this age as they were in the 1960's. The objectification of women throughout our nation and the world and the normalization of extremist racist groups are more prevalent than ever. Prophetic ministry brings comfort to the oppressed and speaks truth to power. Prophetic ministry is fueled by an intense prayer life that is actively engaged in spiritual warfare. Battles must be fought and won in the spirit prior to securing victory in the natural.

WATCHMAN'S MINISTRY

"I have set watchmen on your walls, O Jerusalem; They shall never hold their peace day or night. You who make mention of the Lord, do not keep silent, and give Him no rest till He establishes And till He makes Jerusalem a praise in the earth."

Isaiah 62:6-7

As we focus on the watchman's ministry, we can gain some insight into authentic prophetic ministry. Walls refers to tall, lofty, or elevated places. Watchmen being stationed on the wall gives them an advantage; they have greater visibility of both the inside and outside of the city.

Proper training of a watchman is critical. One of the first requirements of training is the ability to distinguish between the enemies and fellow brethren from a great distance. A trained watchman can discern between a friend and a foe. Once a foe is detected, the watchman cannot keep silent or be passive about its presence. The scripture further says you shall not keep silent, you will never hold your peace day nor night. Watchmen were on duty around the clock. It is a trusted and elevated place that requires keen insight and oversight. As mature intercessors, this level of prayer is of the highest order. As they speak, their voices must be distinct and crystal clear. Not only are they sounding an alarm and readiness for the children of the Lord, they are fervently reminding God of His word until it is manifested in the earth. As the scripture below states:

"And give Him no rest till He establishes and till He makes Jerusalem a praise in the earth."

Isaiah 62:7

TRAVAILING FOR THE LORD

There is no rest for the watchman in ministry. Throughout the entire world, intercessors are constantly praying. This is not being choreographed or scheduled by denominations or reformations, but is solely being orchestrated by the Holy Spirit.

"...For as soon as Zion was in labor, She gave birth to her children."

Isaiah 66:8

The watchman's ministry is one of travailing. Childbirth is never possible without travailing. The birthing process is intense for mother and baby. Apostolic centers have to be marinated in prayer to bring forth what the Lord desires. John the Baptist was crying in the desert, referring to travailing for the Kingdom of God. He travailed and prepared the way for the Lord. His crying consisted of both intercession and proclamation. Our voice in intercession determines the weight of our voice in proclamation. We have to make sure that our proclamation is "not with persuasive words of human wisdom, but in demonstration of the Spirit and of power" (*1 Corinthians 2:4*)

"Now when Abram heard that his brother was taken captive, he armed his three hundred and eighteen trained servants who were born in his own house, and went in pursuit as far as Dan."

Genesis 14:14

When Abram became aware of Lots' captivity, he pursued after him with his trained and armed men. We must take note that

Abram armed only his trained men. To arm an untrained man is very dangerous. To place people in leadership without them going through the training process is dangerous for them, dangerous for the people they will lead, dangerous for the leadership where they serve, and dangerous for the city and community where they serve. No one joins the military without going through basic training. To place someone in military service and equip them when they know little to nothing about weaponry, formation, loyalty, sacrifice, and other vital aspects is detrimental. Can you imagine having them drive a tank, fly a fighter plane, navigate a ship, or possess a machine gun?

We must ensure leadership is properly trained. Just because someone may have been trained or equipped to serve in ministry at another place does not automatically mean that they are equipped to serve at that level of leadership in your ministry. Most people have only been exposed to pastoral lead ministry with very little information or understanding regarding five-fold ministry, which I also refer to as apostolic ministry. Individuals must be trained so that they can understand the order of the vision that they are called to serve in. Also, they must understand the importance of capturing the heart of the leaders that they are assigned to. They must have the mindset and heart of a student or disciple to learn the "ways" of the leaders to whom they are submitting to and serving with. In connection with any apostolic center, the entry must be rooted in humility, not in exhalation. Always be humble and take the low road, instead of trying to get connections to the 'right' people in order to show how 'gifted' and 'anointed' you are. Need I remind you, that in apostolic centers, everyone is gifted, talented, and anointed. One's ability to remain humble and teachable is paramount. Proper training sifts that out. Training matures a house and equips the body for the work of the ministry (*Ephesians 4*)

> *"He divided his forces against them by night, and he and his servants attacked them and pursued them as far as Hobah, which is north of Damascus. So, he brought back all the goods, and also brought back his brother Lot and his goods, as well as the women and the people."*
>
> *Genesis 14:15-16*

During the night, Abram attacked the enemy and rescued everyone as well as their possessions. He interceded for Lot and his possessions. Intercession is one of the major ways for an apostolic team to become synchronized and connected. It is extremely risky to entrust someone who is not fully vested in prayer to a place in leadership within any vision. The ministry of intercession is not only about equipping, training, and arming, but it is also about waging war, conquering, and recovering. By travailing in prayer, you can regain everything that you have lost. You can get back everything that you have lost through the power of intercession. Travailing in prayer, which can manifest in crying, groaning, and intense laboring in His presence, may leave you physically drained and exhausted, but it is better to be empty and poured out in His presence, than to be full and lost. Declare war on the enemy, the victory is already yours.

RUNNING WITH THE VISION

"I will stand my watch and set myself on the rampart (tower), and watch to see what He will say to me, And what I will answer when I am corrected. Then the Lord answered me and said: "Write the vision And make it plain on tablets that he may run who reads it".

Habakkuk 2:1-2

God calls for you to stand up on the tower to travail in the spirit. At the Fountain Gate, you are equipped, developed, and trained for prophetic ministry. The Spirit of the Lord trains and prepares you for this assignment. Training prepares you for vision. Prophetic visionaries must be trained and developed in their sight, hearing, declaring, and writing.

Prophetic people have a unique skillset that enables them to "run". There is a sense of urgency to their assignment. Once again, the vision is not passive. Just as runners, sprinters, and those who run long distance train to execute a successful race with precision, intercessors are developed to move skillfully and swiftly in sync with the Holy Spirit.

"So he shepherded them according to the integrity of his heart, And guided them by the skillfulness of his hands."

Psalm 78:72

"He teaches my hands to make war, so that my arms can bend a bow of bronze."

Psalm 18:34

This means He trains you prophetically. Many people do not understand prophetic training, as they are more familiar and comfortable with traditional pastoral grace that leads them beside still waters, but prophetic grace is radical.

WATCHES OF THE NIGHT

Our prophetic sharpness is activated at the Fountain Gate. Here is where intercessory mantles are released and activated as we are being groomed as watchmen.

> *"The burden against Dumah. He calls to me out of Seir, "Watchman, what of the night? Watchman, what of the night?"*
>
> *Isaiah 21:11*

Time is an important element of the watchman's ministry. Let us first deal with the night. We will find this facet relates to time by going back to the days of creation,

> *"God called the light Day, and the darkness He called Night. So the evening and the morning were the first day."*
>
> *Genesis 1:5*

In the beginning, the earth was formless, and darkness was over the face of the earth. God created light and divided the light from darkness. He called the light day and darkness night; the evening and the morning were the first day. According to God, the cycle for the day does not begin in the morning, but in the evening. This fact is emphasized all throughout the creation; the evening and the morning were the second day (*Gen 1:8*), the evening and the morning were the third day (*Gen 1:13*), the evening and the morning were the fourth day (*Gen 1:19*) and the list continues until the evening and the morning were the sixth day (*Gen 1:31*).

> *"Watch and pray, lest you enter into temptation. The spirit indeed is willing, but the flesh is weak."*
>
> *Mark 14:38*

> *"Praying always with all prayer and supplication in the Spirit, being watchful to this end with all perseverance and supplication for all the saints—"*
>
> *Ephesians 6:18*

Watchmen understand the importance of observation as well as its connection with God. Watchmen are able to discern time and are in rhythm and sync with the Holy Spirit. A watchman must be alert, sharp, and discerning. They must always be on guard and prepared for any unforeseen or unexpected incident or occurrence in the spirit realm. Watching in the scripture means being on guard, being on your post, prepared to do warfare, and always ready to do what God is calling you to do.

Watches of the night refer to four different scheduled timeframes and are based on periods of spiritual activity:

a) The Evening Watch (6pm to 9pm):

The first watch is the evening watch. This is the time for resting and the time you take for yourself to steal away from the anxiety of the day.

"And when He had sent the multitudes away, He went up on the mountain by Himself to pray. Now when evening came, He was alone there."

Matthew 14:23

In this text, we find Jesus alone in the evening praying. He had sent the multitudes away, even His disciples, so that He could spend time alone with the Father. Jesus had a habit of pulling away and setting aside time to seek the Father. He made it a practice to pull away by Himself for periods of time to get rest from the cares of the world. This is a prime example of self-care, a discipline that was lifesaving, along with meditation, during my season of respite. Despite a busy and full schedule of ministry, Jesus was able to regularly spend time alone praying. We must make sure that we are following this example and pattern. Ministry is demanding. Remember, Jethro was deeply concerned about the wear and tear that ministry placed on Moses, his family, and the children of Israel. Jesus pulled away, not only from the crowd, but also from His disciples to refuel and recharge.

Nothing is more crucial than maintaining your personal time with God. This is your time alone to engage with God to be refreshed and renewed. Also, it a time where you are re-energized by being in certain places or engaged in activities that replenish you (i.e.- reading, exercising, personal care). Satan knows that if

he can keep you from having personal and intimate time with the
Father, he can win the battle.

*"This Book of the Law shall not depart from your mouth, but
you shall meditate in it day and night, that you may observe to
do according to all that is written in it. For then you will make
your way prosperous, and then you will have good success."*

Joshua 1:8

Meditation is a vital spiritual discipline in order to live a prosperous and successful life. You must isolate and separate yourself
from the rest of the world. You must find that secret and sacred
place for quiet meditation.

*"In the beginning God created the heavens and the earth. The
earth was without form, and void; and darkness was on the face
of the deep. And the Spirit of God was hovering over the face of
the waters."*

Genesis 1:1-2

In the midst of chaos, confusion, and darkness we observe
how the Spirit of God withdrew, transcended, and hovered over
the chaos from a superior level. This is how I experience meditation. Many shy away from the mere mention of the word
meditation due to a lack of knowledge. Meditation requires you
to unplug from lower levels of chaos and confusion. This must be
a deliberate process. Wherever the "noise" is coming from, you
must silence it by steering your focus away from chaos. You are
guarding the various gates to your heart, especially your eye and
ear gates. Your prophetic acuity will be weakened by seeing and

hearing only on the natural level. Next, we see how the Spirit of God elevated above the chaos. This elevation is done within your spirit and mind by quieting yourself so that you can be at one with your Creator. This is the reality that David experienced when he penned,

"Be still and know that I am God…"

Psalm 46:10

This blessed quietening will allow you to sync with God and with self. It is in this place where your mind is opened to the power of imagination and visualization that exceeds abundantly beyond your natural abilities. Light is then shed within you, to cause you to envision a world that is no longer engrossed with chaos or darkness, but with order, purpose, and light. The result of this meditative experience empowers you to speak from a posture that will create and activate purpose and fulfillment.

b) The Midnight Watch (9 pm to midnight):

The second watch is the midnight watch. This is the time for thanksgiving and intervention.

"But at midnight Paul and Silas were praying and singing hymns to God, and the prisoners were listening to them."

Acts 16:25

"Then Moses said, "Thus says the Lord: 'About midnight I will go out into the midst of Egypt;"

Exodus 11:4

After we have stilled ourselves through meditation, we are now positioned to experience God's glory in the midnight watch. Midnight is the time for divine intervention. This was the time God passed through Egypt to kill the firstborn (*Exodus 11:4*). During the midnight watch, God comes in like the man of war and does warfare on our behalf. It was during the night that God sent the east wind to divide the Red Sea and made the Israelites walk on dry ground. King David rose at midnight to sing praises to the Lord (*Psalm 119:62*). Paul and Silas praised God at midnight, and God intervened and set them free from prison (*Acts 16:25*).

c) The Breaking of Day (Midnight to 3am):

The third watch is the breaking of day. This is the continuation of intense spiritual activity past the midnight watch. Dreams and visions are released during this watch and often times, impartation of counsel and instructions.

"In a dream, in a vision of the night, when deep sleep falls upon men, while slumbering on their beds, then He opens the ears of men, and seals their instructions."

Job 33:15-16

At the same time, during this watch, the enemy tries to throw darts of doubt, confusion, reservation, and hesitation. This can relate to the cock crowing announcing the dawn of another day. It was during this watch of the night that Peter denied Christ three times (*Mark 14*). During this watch of the night, you may experience an attack of tiredness, fatigue, and weariness. During this time seeds of doubt may be sown. The enemy will attempt to wear you down and make you feel as if you cannot go on and complete your assignment. You must always be on guard so that the enemy does not take an upper hand. Again, we are not ignorant of his devices.

d) The Morning Watch (3am to 6am):

"So Abraham rose early in the morning and saddled his donkey, and took two of his young men with him, and Isaac his son; and he split the wood for the burnt offering, and arose and went to the place of which God had told him."

Genesis 22:3

God wanted Abraham to sacrifice his only son Isaac. Abraham never questioned God and he was very submissive to the voice of God. Abraham responded immediately and without delay. He set out early in the morning in pursuit of fulfilling God's will. God expects the same immediate response from each of us. In most of today's households, mornings are very hectic. Our morning needs to be anchored as we intentionally set the foundations for our day.

"Then Jacob rose early in the morning, and took the stone that he had put at his head, set it up as a pillar, and poured oil on top of it."

Genesis 28:18

After experiencing the dream from the Lord, Jacob memorialized the encounter in the morning by taking a stone and establishing it as a pillar, then anointing it with oil. Unlike Abraham, Jacob did not have the time to build an altar there. Jacob could truly attest that,

"...*Weeping may endure for a night, but joy comes in the morning.*"

Psalm 30:5

PROPHETIC TRAINING; HEARING, SEEING, SPEAKING, & WRITING

"*Then Elijah said to Ahab, "Go up, eat and drink; for there is the sound of abundance of rain.*"

I Kings 18:41

"*Son of man, I have made you a watchman for the house of Israel; therefore, hear a word from My mouth, and give them warning from Me.*"

Ezekiel 3:17

- HEARING IN THE SPIRIT

Prophetic training for a watchman includes hearing in the

spirit. Spiritual ears must be developed and matured to tap into the frequency of the Holy Spirit. We have sound waves all around us that allow us to tap into the radio or television frequencies. In the same way, our ear needs to be synchronized to the frequency of the Holy Spirit. Elijah said to King Ahab, "I hear the sound of abundance of rain." Even before he could see any clouds, his spiritual receptacles were tuned in and sharpened enough to hear the sound of rain. Ezekiel says as a watchman, one must hear the Word from the mouth of the Lord. As a young boy, Samuel was ready to open his ears and hear what the Lord had to say. He humbled himself and said, "Speak, for your servant is listening," (*I Sam 3*). Are your ears attentive to hear His voice?

"He who has an ear, let him hear what the Spirit says to the churches."

Revelation 3:13

The enemy is a masterful manipulator. He uses sound, noises, and voices to attempt to drown out God's voice. That is one reason why Satan tries to bring confusion around the discipline of meditation, because meditation eliminates other sounds, voices, and noise and brings God's voice to the forefront. It is through this portal that we are able to hear on a frequency beyond natural hearing.

- SEEING IN THE SPIRIT

"His watchmen are blind, they are all ignorant; They are all

*dumb dogs, They cannot bark; Sleeping, lying down, loving to
slumber."*

Isaiah 56:10

This is a great indictment that Isaiah levies against leaders,
that of blindness and ignorance. They are in leadership positions,
yet they are utterly dysfunctional. They see the natural calami-
ties within our cities and nation, yet they remain unmoved. They
physically see the conditions, yet they are too comfortable and
complacent to travail on a higher realm to see that which the Holy
Spirit desires to employ, which is to bring comfort and vision to
the sightless and hopeless in the natural realm.

*"And when the servant of the man of God arose early and went
out, there was an army, surrounding the city with horses and
chariots. And his servant said to him, "Alas, my master! What
shall we do?" So he answered, "Do not fear, for those who are
with us are more than those who are with them." 17 And Elisha
prayed, and said, "Lord, I pray, open his eyes that he may see."
Then the Lord opened the eyes of the young man, and he saw.
And behold, the mountain was full of horses and chariots of fire
all around Elisha."*

II Kings 6:15-17

In the midst of an apparently hopeless situation, this young
man was operating according to the scope of his experience and
sight. Yet, having a prophetic connection literally shifted his life.
So often we would focus upon this disciple's fear, however, what
speaks loudly to me is the approach he takes in addressing his

prophetic teacher, Elisha. Because of his connection to Elisha and his tutoring, I do not believe that he ever became fearful. He saw the situation and, being a wise student, approached his leader for insight. Elisha, knowing that fear blinds and gives us a distorted perspective, speaks first into his heart, and brings comfort so that this young man would not be immobilized by fear. Then he prays a prophetic prayer to bring insight and enlightenment to this protégé. There are some lessons that experiences will draw out of you with the aid of skilled and mature leadership.

- SPEAKING IN THE SPIRIT

"Put Me in remembrance; Let us contend together; State your case, that you may be acquitted."

Isaiah 43:26

"...For the testimony of Jesus is the spirit of prophecy."

Revelation 19:10

Those at the Fountain Gate are developed and trained to speak new languages. Speaking prophetically requires a sensitivity to what you hear in the Spirit and simply trusting that He will bring to past what you release verbally. Oftentimes you may have never given it any thought, however, there is an unction within you to say what you sense He is saying or what He is feeling during that moment. The testimony of Jesus is the spirit of prophecy. (*Revelation 10:9*) When you speak the word of prophesy, you are releasing a proceeding word. It goes before you! The release of the prophetic word speaks to power and principalities, commanding them to respond to the Word of the Lord. Alignment and manifestation are the results of prophetic utterance.

- WRITING IN THE SPIRIT

"Write the things which you have seen, and the things which are, and the things which will take place after this;"

Revelation 1:19

Documenting or writing the vision will make the prophetic training complete. He says write the vision because when you write it, you give it shape and form. You may forget what you see, hear, and speak in the Spirit, but once you write it, you have a living document that you can use for future reference. Remember, the Fountain Gate is always under severe attack and the enemy is always waiting to rob you of your blessings. Every time you have a vision or hear His voice in the Spirit, the Lord is giving you seed. If you do not write it down, then it can become misplaced seed. We do not have time to misplace seed, so always make a note of what you see, hear, and speak in the spirit. Always be alert because God can reveal Himself at any time. It may be while you are in your bed or while you are walking down the street. Whatever it is, just write down what you see, hear, and speak. Never sleep spiritually but be vigilant always and expect divine visitations.

CHAPTER 7

The Water Gate

THE MINISTRY OF THE WORD

"And all the people gathered themselves together as one man into the street that was before the water gate;..."

Nehemiah 8:1

We have now arrived at the seventh gate, the Water Gate. The Water Gate has many symbolic meanings. First, as the seventh gate, it is biblically symbolic of completion. The number seven represents divine completion or divine perfection. We find many references to this throughout the Word of God:

- In Genesis, creation took seven days to manifest
- In Revelation, there are seven churches of Asia Minor
- In Acts, the deacon's ministry began with seven

The Water Gate is symbolic of completion and perfection, but it also represents the Word of God. According to Nehemiah 3:26, this gate did not need to be repaired. The fact is, you cannot add to the Word nor can you take away from the Word. To get a

foundational understanding of what takes place at the Water Gate,
look at Nehemiah,

> *"Now all the people gathered together as one man in the open*
> *square that was in front of the Water Gate; and they told Ezra*
> *the scribe to bring the Book of the Law of Moses, which the Lord*
> *had commanded Israel. So Ezra the priest brought the Law*
> *before the assembly of men and women and all who could hear*
> *with understanding on the first day of the seventh month. Then*
> *he read from it in the open square that was in front of the Water*
> *Gate from morning until midday, before the men and women*
> *and those who could understand; and the ears of all the people*
> *were attentive to the Book of the Law.*
>
> *So Ezra the scribe stood on a platform of wood which they had*
> *made for the purpose; and beside him, at his right hand, stood*
> *Mattithiah, Shema, Anaiah, Urijah, Hilkiah, and Maaseiah;*
> *and at his left hand Pedaiah, Mishael, Malchijah, Hashum,*
> *Hashbadana, Zechariah, and Meshullam. And Ezra opened the*
> *book in the sight of all the people, for he was standing above all*
> *the people; and when he opened it, all the people stood up. And*
> *Ezra blessed the Lord, the great God.*
>
> *Then all the people answered, "Amen, Amen!" while lifting up*
> *their hands. And they bowed their heads and worshiped the*
> *Lord with their faces to the ground."*
>
> *Nehemiah 8:1-6*

Here we find that the walls and the gates have been complet-
ed. Israel had just come out of Babylonian captivity, which was

one of the darkest times in their history.

"For there those who carried us away captive asked of us a song,
And those who plundered us requested mirth, Saying, "Sing us
one of the songs of Zion!"

How shall we sing the Lord's song In a foreign land?"

Psalm 137:3-4

Even though their captivity was long, painful, and harsh,
the children of Israel returned home to restore the temple under
Zerubbabel's leadership. Nehemiah was used as an apostolic leader in rebuilding the walls and in establishing the gates.

Ezra, the priest, was responsible for re-establishing the release
of the Word of God. While in bondage, the children of Israel lost
their appreciation for the Word of God. They had totally drifted
away from God's Word during their time of exile. They had lost
their understanding of the Word of God and the revelation of
who God was.

RETURNING HOME

After being in a place of bondage for so long, some of the
people had forgotten about God or believed that God had forgotten about them. Upon arriving home, they realized they needed
a change of heart and a change of mind. They did not want to
go back to the same situation they had just come from. Their
goal became not to establish governmental rule for themselves,
but to find God again. They were solely focused on hearing and

receiving the Word of God. Their first priority was to seek a place of repentance and to place a demand on the Word of God to be released over their lives.

Remember the ten lepers and how God healed every last one of them, but only one came back to acknowledge Him and thank Him for what He had done (*Luke 17*)? You must come back home with the right mind, the right attitude, and the right heart. When the children of Israel came back, there were no welcome home banners with balloons and food and celebrating. That was not the first thing on the hearts and minds of those that were rooted in the faith. Their priority was to get to the Water Gate where they could honor the Word of God.

Nehemiah 8:1 states, "*And all the people gathered themselves together as one man.*" They had been through the bondage and the pain of captivity, and now they were home and all came to one meeting place to hear the Word of God. It says all, not some but all, the people gathered together. Declare and decree the Word of God over your household,

"*...But as for me and my house, we will serve the LORD.*"

Joshua 24:15

"*Not forsaking the assembling of ourselves together, as is the manner of some, but exhorting one another, and so much the more as you see the Day approaching.*"

Hebrews 10:25

GATHERING AND ASSEMBLING

There is significance to the word assembling. When we read about not forsaking the assembling of ourselves, people think that means we should come together in a church setting. Regular attendance should benefit believers in their spiritual development, as well as the opportunity to be in fellowship with one another. We should be faithful in our attendance; however, COVID-19 has shown us that church is larger than physically being together, that is only a part of it. According to *Nehemiah 8:1*, they gathered first and then they were assembled. The gathering anointing deals with bringing people together, but you can be together and not be assembled.

Apostolic centers are places where God gathers His people to connect with one another and to pursue destiny. Individuals are drawn to these centers because they possess a gathering anointing. There is a magnetic pull that causes those who are assigned to the vision to be drawn in. People will come and desire to be a part of these centers. The anointing that's upon these centers will draw individuals. They will be gathered from near and far, not just physically, but through social media and internet platforms. They understand that it is a life-altering Word being released and modeled. This is the gathering anointing at work.

Gathering is the initial phase. We can use a jigsaw puzzle as an analogy. A jigsaw puzzle has many pieces; let's say five hundred pieces. While in the box, all the pieces are gathered, but they are not assembled. The puzzle becomes assembled when you take the pieces out of the box and you fit and join them together. To be assembled is to be in your appointed place. When proper assembly takes place, you will be able to receive what is needed for your life as well as being able to release the assignment that God has placed on your life. That is when you are able to make an impartation into the body from what God has empowered and developed within you. Impartation works both ways; God imparts gifts to you so that you can impart them back to the body of Christ and to the world.

"For because of Him the whole body (the church, in all its various parts), closely joined and firmly knit together by the joints and ligaments with which it is supplied, when each part [with power adapted to its need] is working properly [in all its functions], grows to full maturity, building itself up in love."

Ephesians 4:16 AMP

A part of your kingdom assignment is to aid in releasing the vision where you are connected. Your kingdom assignment also expands well beyond the realm of your local church to the marketplace. Ministry cannot be restricted to the four walls of our buildings. God uses and develops you in the soil into which you were planted.

UNITY OF THE BODY

In Nehemiah Chapter 8, the Word says they were together as one man. This symbolizes unity. There will never be a release of a prophetic Word of God in the midst of confusion and disarray. In the book of *Ezekiel 37*, the Lord has Ezekiel prophesy to bones that were disjointed and disconnected. Ezekiel was instructed to prophecy to the bones and, because of his prophecy, the bones came together and were assembled. We need to understand the importance of unity and what is needed to protect unity.

"Now I plead with you, brethren, by the name of our Lord Jesus Christ, that you all speak the same thing, and that there be no divisions among you, but that you be perfectly joined together in the same mind and in the same judgment."

I Corinthians 1:10

"Behold, how good and how pleasant it is for brethren to dwell together in unity!"

Psalm 133:1

Any organization that is not operating in unity will be draining to the people and will be greatly delayed in its purpose. There will never be a full release of the Word of God in a disconnected and disjointed church.

"One Lord, one faith, one baptism;"

Ephesians 4:5

Regardless of your title or position, we are all one body. We are brought into the Kingdom of God as a unified body. So often individuals will attempt to sow discord to disconnect you from your assigned place through division. It is just one of the many tactics that the enemy will try to use to uproot you from your assigned place. Every time you recognize and gain understanding of the devices he is using, he loses ground in your life.

"Lest Satan should take advantage of us: for we are not ignorant of his devices."

II Corinthians 2:11

One of the ways Satan can take advantage of you is when you are unaware of his devices, plots, ploys and plans. The devil is a liar! The authority of God's Word is the only thing that's going to last. You have to get under the Word of God and submit to it. You have to understand, comprehend and recognize the order of God, realizing that "God is not the author of confusion," (*I Corinthians 14:33*). When we recognize and understand that God is a God of order, we realize that the Water Gate is where the heart of God is released, the order of God is released, and the mind of God is released through His Word.

HONOR THE WORD

There must first be an honoring of the Word of God. The children of Israel experienced what it was like to live in bondage, captivity, darkness, and fear. When they were finally freed, the first thing they wanted to do was to hear the Word of the Lord. Ezra is on a pulpit not to lift himself up, but to lift up the Word of God. There is significance to the pulpit. The pulpit carries the impetus to pull up out of the pit. When the Word of God is released from the pulpit, it will pull you up out of situations; the heartaches and trials that you've been going through. The Word of God has so much power and authority that it can reach down into the pit and pull you out. The pulpit is to be used to declare the Word of the Lord. The pulpit is symbolic of the place where the Word of God receives honor.

When the people said to Ezra, "bring the book", they were not asking for the latest novel or the written philosophies of men. They were not looking for the New York Times best sellers or the trendiest topic in the city. They wanted and expected Ezra to bring The Book, the Word of the Most High God. Thank God for The Book. When you truly honor the Book, it will prevent you from going through many trials and tribulations, as well as comfort you during those times. God's Word will let you know He is concerned about where you are and that He has a plan and purpose for your life.

Your feelings are meaningful. You should value the counsel and opinion of those who are close and dear to you. Yet the final authority in your life should be the Word of God. Jesus said,

"...'Man shall not live by bread alone, but by every word that proceeds from the mouth of God.'"

Matthew 4:4

Thank God for the various voices in our lives, from friends to family to professionals, however the question remains, whose report will you believe? Hear the report of the Lord. I know what the professionals have said, but I want you to know that the Word of God is the final authority. Thank God for professionals and all of their training and their skill set, however their knowledge is still limited by their humanity. We all "know in part".

The Bible is more than a historical book; it is the very heart of God. The Word of God says,

> *"In all your ways acknowledge Him and He shall direct your paths,"*
>
> *Proverbs 3:6*

Whatever dilemma you may be facing today, if you would honor and acknowledge that God is still on the throne, the enemy has no choice but to back up. Tell the enemy he is a liar. Let him know that he has no authority over your family, over your mind, or over your finances.

> *"And they overcame him by the blood of the Lamb and by the word of their testimony, and they did not love their lives to the death."*
>
> *Revelation 12:11*

In apostolic centers, the Word that is coming forth is more than just a sermon, it's a proceeding Word that will properly propel you into your assignment, it's a Word that will bring transformation and elevation to your life. Therefore, when coming to the Word you bring a spirit of expectancy knowing that you will have an encounter with the True and Living God; totally different from the usual and familiar.

The Word of God is vibrant and alive. His Word will endure forever. Regardless of how people try to discredit and dishonor

His Word, it still stands. God's Word says,

> *"Heaven and earth will pass away, but My words will by no means pass away,"*
>
> *Matthew 24:35*

His Word must govern us daily. David, the sweet psalmist of Israel, said, *"Your (His) word is a lamp to my feet and a light to my path"*. Even in the midst of leading a growing and energetic congregation, leaders cannot be swayed by the latest trends and fads of "Christianity". Emotions run high and trends are fleeting. Yet Apostolic leaderships are able to navigate through all of the "smoke screens" with penetrating precision, based on His word. When making decisions, whether personal, professional, or ministerial, His Word will release a peace on matters with instructions and directions pertaining to your assignment.

ATTENTIVE TO THE WORD

> *"My son, give attention to my words; Incline your ear to my sayings. Do not let them depart from your eyes; Keep them in the midst of your heart; For they are life to those who find them, And health to all their flesh. Keep your heart with all diligence, For out of it spring the issues of life."*
>
> *Proverbs 4:20-23*

So often, our minds are preoccupied with other things, from financial concerns to taking care of an aging loved one. As we prepare to have an encounter with God, we need worship to be a time to focus and to draw our attention to The Living God as we prepare to honor God by giving attention to His Word. If one is easily distracted from simply hearing God's Word, then you can only imagine how easily distracted one will be when trying to honor God daily when you consider the busyness of life. You have to be attentive and prepared for His word. Worship sets the atmosphere as you focus upon the Lord. Not only in public, but privately we must set atmospheres of worship in our homes so that He may dwell with us. Again, recognize the devices of the enemy. This worship atmosphere will posture us to attend or to "lean in" to His Word as it is released. The enemy knows if he can keep us distracted or cause us not to honor God's Word; he can keep us from reaching our appointed destiny.

You must take authority over the distractions and tactics of the enemy. The maneuver of the enemy is to keep your mind occupied with everything except for God's Word. He will use the past to keep you focused on your mistakes, causing you to live with a deep sense of condemnation, regret, and shame. He will attempt to sabotage your future with anxiety, fear, or prompting you to overanalyze every Word God has given you.

"Casting down arguments and every high thing that exalts itself against the knowledge of God, bringing every thought into captivity to the obedience of Christ,"

II Corinthians 10:5

When you give attention to the Word of God and what He says, not only will you find life, but you will find health and prosperity too. Hallelujah! When you come focused on the Word of God, you're going to leave healthy. You will leave with a renewed mind. You will leave with the joy of the Lord instead of the burden of sadness or the cloak of heaviness. They will be exchanged for the joy of the Lord and the garment of praise. There are benefits when you give attention to the Word of God, especially at the Water Gate. God brings order, strength, prosperity, and health to your life. Not only are we to attend to His Words, He then instructs us to incline our ears. He's talking about tilting and leaning your ears forward to hear what the Lord is saying. That demonstrates a sense of expectancy. When you incline, you are on the edge of your seat leaning in to hear what thus says the Lord.

You don't posture yourself to recline. You do not come to lean away from the Word. You come to lean into the Word. Your posture isn't casually laid back with no expectation or honor. You approach His Word with an inclination and an expectation that God is going to do something just for you. If your heart is not inclined you may find yourself in a position of recline, which will lead to a decline in your passion for the things of God. You want to know why you aren't passionate about the things of God? Maybe it's because you are in a posture that is reclined and drawn back from Him.

FOCUS ON THE WORD

The preaching of the Word of God is not an oratorical activity that sounds good, used to stroke our emotions. The Word comes with the power to change your life forever. A worship experience means you are participating by inclining your ear and being sensitive to the Holy Spirit. The pulpit is not a place of entertainment. It is a sacred place, where God intends to have His heart and mind released. Whenever you encounter the Word of God, you must come with an inclined ear to God's Word. They want and need to hear a Word that will send them back to their lives with purpose. Placing a demand upon the Word of God will bring insight, directions, and encouragement to your life and kingdom assignment.

"... 'Lord, if it is You, command me to come to You on the water.'"
Matthew 14:28

When Peter said this, his focus was on the Lord. As long as he was focused on Jesus, The Living Word, he was able to walk on the water. It was not until Peter got distracted by the wind, and took his eyes off Jesus, that he began to sink. The wind had been blowing the entire time, however it was not until Peter turned his focus to the distraction, that he began to lose it. We have to train and discipline ourselves so that we won't get distracted by the activities surrounding us, nor by focusing on the storms of life. Keep your mind on God's Word. Stay focused on Him. What I can say with confidence is that the storm that you are going through will not last.

"Looking unto Jesus, the author and the finisher of our faith, ... "
Hebrews 12:2

In the midst of the corporate anointing, whenever a proceeding Word is being released, God can and will speak a word designed and targeted just for you. We serve a God that's so awesome and powerful that He takes a right now Word and strategically finds you, right where you are and meets your need.

DO THE WORD

> *"Now it shall come to pass, if you diligently obey the voice of the Lord your God, to observe carefully all His commandments which I command you today, that the Lord your God will set you high above all nations of the earth. 2 And all these blessings shall come upon you and overtake you, because you obey the voice of the Lord your God:"*
>
> *Deuteronomy 28:1-2*

The King James Version says, *"Hearken diligently unto the voice of the Lord thy God."* To hearken diligently is not just about hearing the Word. Biblically, hearken means not only to hear, but also to do. Growing up, when my mother wanted us to do something, she didn't ask us to do it, she told us to do it. If for some reason we didn't do it, she would say, "Didn't you hear me?" She was the only adult voice in the house, so of course we heard her. What was evident is that she had the revelation of hearkening because she would then say, "Evidently you didn't hear me, because if you had, you would have done what I told you to do."

That's exactly what God is asking, "If you hear Me, why aren't you doing what I told you to do?" God is saying, "If you hear Me, do it!" God is saying, "I have released The Word over your life and the grace to empower you to do what I am commanding you to do." God is not giving you good ideas; He is giving you God ideas. He is giving plans and thoughts for your destiny, for your children, for your marriage, for your finances, for your business, and for your lineage. God will never tell you to do a thing and not release sufficient grace for you to carry it out. Every Word that He releases over your life has the grace for you to activate that Word.

God told Abraham to take his only son and offer him as a sacrifice (*Genesis 22*). God knew that Abraham heard Him, and He gave him sufficient grace to take his only son to be a burnt offering. Our problem is that we are trying to make sense of what God wants us to do. Trying to follow God based on your own understanding will get you in trouble every time. The Word of God says,

"Trust in the LORD with all thine heart; and lean not unto thine own understanding,"

Proverbs 3:5

Yet God's Word and revelation is released on a need to know basis. He tells Abraham to go to unfamiliar land and offer his son, Isaac, on a mountain that He will reveal to him. Not only is revelation released on a need to know basis, it is also progressive.

"For whoever has, to him more will be given, and he will have abundance; but whoever does not have, even what he has will be taken away from him."

Matthew 13:12

How can you expect God to continuously give you insights or directions if you have not obeyed the last Word that He has given? When God gave a Word to Jonah, He expected him to carry it out; however, Jonah didn't obey God's Word and he paid for it (*Jonah 1-3*). You will pay for disobedience when you don't obey the Word of God. On the other hand, when you obey God, He pays. God will never short-change you and He will never owe you a thing. Everything God commands and puts before you to do, He will provide all that's needed to accomplish. If you disobey, that means you will have to pay. Trust me on this one: the price you will pay is one you cannot afford.

The Israelites not only gathered and assembled to hear and receive the Word of God, but they also obeyed the Word of God. I believe the major reason and cause for them going into disobedience was a prolonged period of not hearing the Word of God. If that was the case for the Israelites, this may well be the case for your situation or dilemma. Perhaps you are not hearing or doing the Word of God. I want to ask you this, why are you in the situation or dilemma you are in right now? Are you hearing and doing the Word of God?

"If you are willing and obedient, You shall eat the good of the land;"

Isaiah 1:19

Understand that disobedience is sin. You have to make up your mind and tell yourself, "No matter what happens, I will follow God." You see, it's an act of your will. God is not going to force you to do anything. You have to will to trust God; you have to will to serve God. It's not enough just to be willing, but now you have to obey and do! That's why we come to the Water Gate; to hear what God is saying and then do it. At the Water Gate the Word brings refreshing, rejuvenating, cleansing, and purifying.

Amos Chapter 8 talks about a famine in the land. He is not talking about a famine of food, but a famine of the Word of God. Apostolic leaders are not assigned to make you feel good, but to release the Word of God to instruct and to provoke you to good works. As the Word of God is released, your heart should become opened to receive the Word of God. The Word of God in Acts has this to say about the believers,

> *"...they received the word with all readiness, and searched the Scriptures daily to find out whether these things were so."*
>
> *Acts 17:11*

The aim of anointed preaching and teaching is to instruct and to inspire the hearers to execute their kingdom assignment.

CHAPTER 8

The Horse Gate

THE PLACE OF SUPPORT

"Beyond the Horse Gate the priests made repairs, each in front of his own house."

Nehemiah 3:28

The Horse Gate deals with the ministry of support. This includes the components necessary to properly and skillfully aide in the carrying out and execution of the vision.

We often talk and share about five-fold ministry (Ephesians 4) and the various gifting, graces, and anointing released through the five-fold. Paul also identifies another list of ministry gifts that are set in the church as well.

"And God has appointed these in the church: first apostles, second prophets, third teachers, after that miracles, then gifts of healings, helps, administrations, varieties of tongues."

I Corinthians 12:28

We are all a part of the body of Christ and, in-turn, members of His body. As a member of the body, God has an appointed place and an assignment specifically for you. He has assigned the members of His body, the church, various roles. Some are apostles, some are prophets and some are teachers. Some are miracle workers; some have the gift of healing and some the gift of helping. Some are gifted in the area of administration and some uniquely set in as communicators. Having been in ministry for four decades, I value and have a greater appreciation for those who are particularly graced and called to support the ministry. These individuals handle the detailing aspects.

MINISTRY OF HELPS

"And the Lord God said, "It is not good that man should be alone; I will make him a helper comparable to him."

Genesis 2:18

Adam was alone in the garden. God said that it was not good for man to be alone; therefore, He created Eve to be his helper. We are never assigned to carry out a vision from God alone. As a relational God, it is His aim for us to have helpers to aid in carrying out the vision. The ministry of helps is manifested in several ways.

Oftentimes help is supplied from persons within the vision. The Bible tells us that Eve was created from the rib of Adam, meaning taken from the inside. This component of the ministry of helps serves as the apostolic ribs. These individuals are anointed and equipped to provide much needed support to the vision. Some of these helpers may come from inside the vision, such as individuals who have been birthed, nurtured, and groomed from within the ministry. Others may be individuals assigned to your vision, but may not be based within your ministry. They may live in other states or nations, yet they are fully connected to you as their apostolic leader. This symbiotic relationship entails apostolic leaders to impart wisdom, insight, and support to these individuals as they are actively engaged in executing their kingdom assignment wherever they may be located or serving. Simultaneously, these helpers can provide and aide your ministry; through possessing the gifts, talents, and the skill sets to impart what has been entrusted to them to support the vision of the apostolic leader.

When being placed within a local ministry, one should be flexible and willing to serve in whatever capacity is needed. You may be a phenomenal musician; however, the need may be in the media or adult ministry. You may be a marketing wiz; however, there may be a need in the area of administration. Being faithful and diligent in the areas of need will allow your gifts to come to the surface without having to jockey or bargain for position. The greater need is for the vision to be released, not for your personal vision for "your ministry" to be seen. Your heart is shown through your demonstration of faithfulness, excellence, and willingness. Once an opportunity becomes available in your desired ministry area, you may be called to serve there.

As one matures in their spiritual walk, there is a shift of

perspectives. Typically, the initial focus is on how the vision can help you and what the vision can offer you. You are looking to fulfil your needs and desires. Later in your journey, there should be a shift where you begin to look for opportunities where you can offer and share of yourself to make the vision more effective. This is a phenomenal place to be in relationship with the vision: where the relationship is mutually beneficial for all parties. When the vision is effective, so too are the helpers assigned to it. Individuals at this place along the journey are not just receiving, but are now supplying to the body. There are two types of helps: the natural and the spiritual. Both are necessary for different reasons and assignments.

NATURAL HELPS

"…Elisha the son of Shaphat is here, who poured water on the hands of Elijah."

II Kings 3:11

Elisha poured water on the hands of Elijah. This exemplifies the natural help. Natural help is needed in every apostolic center. Every task ought not to require financial compensation. Help in the natural can consist of everything from property maintenance to serving as an assistant in the office. There is a designated time and place when the service is in such a demand, that compensation should be considered. From setting up equipment to serving refreshments, are all considered natural help. This is pivotal for a safe, clean, and healthy atmosphere so that the ministry functions and services can take place seamlessly.

There is also a need for the apostolic leader to have as much liberty as possible, so that they can be absolutely free to serve God, the church, and the community. Based upon the demands that the servant of God has, there should be an individual or a team of individuals who assist in the various natural needs of the leader. For example, if the leader travels on a regular basis, when possible, these individuals should assist if it is financially feasible for them to do so. Over the years, I have been fortunate to have some awesome men who willingly served me while ministering in late night services on the rural roads of Virginia to traveling overseas in Nigeria and India while ministering to thousands. They attended to my needs solely because they understood the need for me to be free and rested to minister as needed.

The very first individuals to aid me in ministry while I served as Pastor at Mt. Nebo Baptist Church in West Point Virginia were two elderly retired gentlemen, Sterling Edwards and John Thompson. Both were in their seventies at that time and became deacons during my pastorate. I was a young 29-year-old pastor at the time after being "voted" into what was recognized as one of the top rural churches in America. These two gentlemen, both old enough to be my grandfather, lovingly served me because they felt it was their call to help. They wanted to make sure I would not need to do anything that they were able and willing to do. Whenever they found out that I went to an event by myself, they both would fuss with me. While working on my master's degree on Fridays and

Saturdays at Virginia Union University School of Theology, Deacon Sterling would stay awake until he saw my car pulling in front of the church parsonage around midnight. After many road trips and services, they both knew the fatigue that I encountered from having a young family, pastoring, attending school, and all that came with it. We shared great moments and lifelong memories of our time together.

They sought neither visibility nor a sense of entitlement. They just made my heavy load considerably lighter. As my ministry grew and the demand rapidly increased, I have been extremely fortunate to have an intimate group of awesome men who have served and freed me naturally to remain totally focused on my ministry assignment. What has been amazing is that these individuals not only attended to the needs of my family and me, but they have become family. This group, with the full support and blessings of their wives, not only attended to my wellbeing, but they also provided spiritual support. From Larry Parson, a retired military officer to William Phillips, who, with the gracious support of his wife Rebecca has been my lead armorbearer for the last decade. The level of support that I have received over these three decades has been invaluable. I am so grateful for every one of these men and their supportive wives for the diligent care that they have provided to me personally. These men willingly sacrificed their time to make sure that I would be as free as possible to provide energetic and vibrant leadership to those I was entrusted to serve, just as Elisha ensured the wellbeing of Elijah. He did not want his man of God to grow weary.

ARMOR BEARERS

"After the death of Moses the servant of the Lord, it came to pass that the Lord spoke to Joshua the son of Nun, Moses' assistant, saying:"

Joshua 1:1

"So Elisha turned back from him, and took a yoke of oxen and slaughtered them and boiled their flesh, using the oxen's equipment, and gave it to the people, and they ate. Then he arose and followed Elijah, and became his servant."

1 Kings 19:21

"So his armorbearer said to him, 'Do all that is in your heart. Go then; here I am with you, according to your heart.'"

1 Samuel 14:7

By serving the man or woman of God, you become a support in that ministry. Joshua was a support for Moses before and after his death; Joshua was assigned to lead the Israelites across the river Jordan into the Promised Land. Elisha was of great aide to Elijah both naturally and spiritually. As a result, he inherited a double portion of the spirit that was on Elijah. The armor bearer of Jonathan followed his leader and was of great support to him in routing the Philistines.

The basic duty of the armor bearer is to aid the Apostolic leader by serving as an attendant in order to keep the leader as free as possible to minister and to serve with as few distractions as possible. The scope of the needs will vary based on the size of the ministry and the leader's schedule. These armor bearers are personal attendants, providing aid to the apostolic leaders. Even though many outside observers would think that this is a glorious "position," those who faithfully serve understand the level of sacrifice and service this ministry requires. Not visible, but behind the scenes, these individuals attend to the needs of the apostolic leaders, whether they are pastors, CEO's, agency leaders or marketplace leaders.

Some leaders may be serving and providing oversight to various ministries and organizations, requiring a more complex infrastructure, while others may be serving in a ministry where the structure is not as demanding. My armor bearers were not only aware of my personal needs but also acted as my security detail. Having a national platform attracted a variety of individuals and not everyone was necessarily supportive. Even more so now, with the racial and political tensions at an all-time high, I strongly recommend security for those who are on the front line of warfare, addressing matters that unearth violent spirits that have long been dormant. Armor bearers must always be accessible to the apostolic leader on short notice. Because of the heavy demand, I had a team who served on a rotating basis. They had to be extremely watchful and prayerful so that I was able to minister effectively without being concerned about anything else. Equally as important, these individuals must be trustworthy. Conversations I had, whether with pastors who were struggling with issues or others sharing the deepest pains of their lives, were often unplanned or impromptu. There were times when my armor bearers were privy to these conversations and had to keep what they heard in the strictest of confidence.

SPIRITUAL HELPS

"But now bring me a musician. Then it happened, when the musician played, that the hand of the Lord came upon him."

II Kings 3:15

"Then the Spirit of the Lord will come upon you, and you will prophesy with them and be turned into another man."

I Samuel 10:6

It is impossible to get into the new dimension by yourself. Elisha needed to get in the presence of the Lord, so he called for the musician to help him to get into his prophetic flow. Elisha needed help, but not just any kind of help, he summoned for spiritual help. Likewise, we find Saul coming into the company of prophets and he turned into another man. The prophetic aid and assistance provoked his change. The change was so noticeable that the text noted it as follows, *"And it happened, when all who knew him formerly saw that he indeed prophesied among the prophets, that the people said to one another, "What is this that has come upon the son of Kish? Is Saul also among the prophets?"* Without any spiritual help and helpers, you may never walk into higher dimensions of the spiritual realm.

APOSTOLIC TEAM

Over the years, I have been privileged to have some phenomenal ministry gifts to collaborate with on apostolic teams. This team consisted of mature and gifted leaders who worked together in helping us to grow, guide, and govern our ministry as well as our network of churches and businesses. It required a great level of mutual respect and honor, as well as having keen insight to understand what gift was needed at a particular time. Whatever grace and gifts were needed, the Lord has placed great favor upon my life to be able to reach out to various team members who were fully engaged with my assignment and able to sharpen and release my vision to new realms. More than just being some of the leading voices in the kingdom, these individuals carried the weight of God upon their lives. Their metron or "measure of rule" varied from regional to national to global.

One of the major decisions that I have made was in the creation of an apostolic council. Many ministries have one person that they submit their ministry to for counsel and wisdom. I understand the essence of that, however, I knew with the scope of my ministry that I needed different voices who could impart and aide in sharing their unique gifting and experience from a global perspective. This apostolic council consisted of international ministry gifts as well as national lawyers who not only kept abreast of church laws, but were also knowledgeable in entrepreneurship. All these individuals were well exposed and extremely relevant in ministry and business affairs. My ministry was extremely complex and varied, with apostolic and prophetic dimensions, in addition to also having business ventures. This consisted of owning a 100,000 square foot shopping mall with businesses leasing from our for-profit arm created apart from the church. We also had a licensed counseling agency, daycare center, transitional housing, a publishing company, and a media component that produced our weekly local and international broadcasts. It was paramount that we connect ourselves with some of the sharpest minds available to us in order for us to be a cutting-edge ministry.

ELDERSHIP

"For this reason I left you in Crete, that you should set in order the things that are lacking, and appoint elders in every city as I commanded you— if a man is blameless, the husband of one wife, having faithful children not accused of dissipation or insubordination."

Titus 1:5-6

Apostle Paul had two major spiritual sons, Timothy and Titus. Essentially, the pastoral epistle, consisting of Corinthians and Titus, are letters to help his sons in ministry to serve the churches properly within Corinth and Crete. Paul speaks of the appointment of elders for several reasons. Firstly, since Paul had departed from Crete, it was important that he leave a trusted and capable leader who could represent and carry out his vison. The leader whom Paul trusted fully was a young spiritual son by the name of Titus. This son was not there to create his own vision, but to further extend and expand Paul's vision. It is pivotal that those appointed to leadership understand that their assignment is to carry out the apostle's vision while he or she is executing their assignment in other places. Titus was placed there by the apostle to represent Paul, not as a replacement. Oversight was always in the hands and under the spiritual jurisdiction of Apostle Paul. Titus understood this and was faithful in the daily operations and pastoral duties.

It is important that we talk about apostolic oversight. Paul was responsible to the Lord to ensure that the believers had a competent pastor (elder) who could adequately meet the needs of the congregation, from feeding them spiritually to protecting them from erroneous teaching. Once again, Titus is there as a servant of God and as a son of Paul. Above all, that relationship must be mutually trusting and committed to the vision of the visionary: Paul.

Having created and birthed ministries, it is important for a clear understanding of apostolic authority and oversight. Those lines, duties, and expectations must be clearly defined so that all parties understand and are in agreement with these dynamics. Having these discussed and properly documented benefits all parties. When these lines are blurred, it can cause great damage to all; the apostle, the pastor, and the church as a whole. It is for this reason that I highly recommend that anytime there is a placement or a transition within any apostolic center, legal documentation should be drawn up and agreed to by the parties involved. Life happens, as well as the realization that people and situations change; that is to be expected. However, to maintain the integrity and the furthering of ministry, I recommend securing legal documentation, especially as a part of succession planning. This will ensure that the agreement is properly carried out. I am sure there are some individuals who would oppose any legal documentation because of the spiritual nature of these relationships. However, even naturally, legal documentation is necessary to transfer property or ownership from a parent to a child. While the legality of that relationship is unquestioned, to ensure proper transfer, legal documentation must be provided.

I strongly recommend this every time a pastor (elder) is placed in position to serve a body, especially if they are placed there apostolically. Their placement is at the behest of the apostle and/ or the governing body. The agreement serves as a supporting document to the placement and describes the inherent details. It serves as a vehicle used by all parties to understand boundaries and responsibilities properly. A pastor who has been placed as a leader over a congregation, within an apostolic structure, must have the liberty to exercise their creativity and individuality. They must be more than just a "hired servant", but someone who is fully aware of the expectations that functioning within an apostolic structure entails. That placement is solely to carry out the vision of the apostle, while ensuring that the pastor has the needed personal space to express their individuality.

Some individuals are wired to function and effectively serve within the context of someone else's vision and some individuals are not. Individuality is a vital part of everyone's calling and space must be granted for each one to express uniqueness, within the scope of the vision. It is just that simple. However, this may not be known until a person is afforded that opportunity. Therefore, the spiritual relationship must be properly maintained with integrity and authenticity. Shared communication by all parties makes this assessment crucial as the assignment is carried out. When a pastor is no longer able to serve in that capacity, then the activation of a separation should take place according to the legal documentation that was agreed upon by all parties when initially enacted. Change is never easy for anyone; however, the aim should be for the transition to take place as smoothly as possible. All parties involved should benefit in such a way that the individual leaving the position is not severed from the relationship. Having open and honest communication throughout the process helps avoid an abrupt ending. This would also give ample time and opportunity for all parties to transition into the next phase of their journey while honoring the opportunity afforded.

Those who have been faithful in serving within an apostolic structure who desire to create a totally new and independent work, should whole-heartedly receive the blessing and financial support as they embark upon their passion. That should be included in the legal documentation, so that individuals who served faithfully are honored financially as they transition in their lives. In doing so, as a caregiver of an apostle's assignment, that vision should be returned into the hands of the apostle who placed the pastor in that position. This is what Paul speaks about when he says *"not building on another's foundation" (Romans 15:20).* Titus was not placed in Crete to execute his ministry, but to represent and to carry out Paul's ministry. That was the sole aim of Paul placing Titus in Crete.

Paul's apostolic assignment gave space for Titus' insight and gifting by releasing him to address whatever was lacking and in need of attention in Crete. Titus was fully qualified in Paul's eyes to bring structure and teaching to those who were in Crete. Titus was given authority to appoint elders within every city there. We see the liberty and authority given to Titus. Paul charges Titus to carry out these assignments.

UNDERSTANDING APOSTLESHIP AND THE BISHOPRIC

For some, Titus could represent the pastoral appointment. He could also represent the appointment of the bishopric. I will use my experience as an example. For years, I was a part of a network alliance that I connected to in 1998. This network had several hundred churches and ministers affiliated throughout the world. In 1999, I was selected by the presiding bishop to serve as a Presbyter and, in 2003, I was consecrated as a bishop within that organization. Whether as a presbyter or bishop, my sole responsibility was to represent the presiding bishop whenever the assignment called for it. This meant meeting with pastors and leaders from the network and ministering in the various churches as requested by him or by invitation of the individual pastors. I served in these capacities while having my own independent apostolic network. I understood fully that my placement and assignment was to support the structure and vision that he had established.

In various denominations, the bishopric may serve as a representative over a geographical region or over a particular department such as missions. Even within these structures, the "regional" bishop has liberty and governmental oversight. However, they still serve under the oversight of the Presiding Bishop.

Within the network that I established, I was responsible for the total operation. This network consisted of five-fold ministerial gifts, congregations, and marketplace entrepreneurs. Our leadership structure had designated individuals serving as liaisons who provided ongoing training and communications with those who were connected. These liaisons represented my apostolic authority. They were placed in these positions because of their commitment, loyalty, and ability to facilitate and to expand the vision.

This network was totally autonomous. Even though I served as a bishop structurally within another network under the vision of the presiding bishop, I also served as an apostle in the network that I created. The flow of my network was significantly different, due to me having complete oversight and liberty. The point I want to reiterate is that the flow was completely different. In the first structure, I served having been placed in that capacity, whereas I had created the other structure. There never was a blending because I understood the boundaries, even though they were never voiced or documented. There was potential for lines to be crossed, however, I knew and respected what I was personally accountable for as well as how I was called to assist. Each structure afforded me the opportunity for growth and both required my faithfulness to the required capacity.

For me, the apostolic assignment is an anointing of pioneering and trail blazing in uncharted realms. It embodies the mantle to create and to establish. The bishopric, in my personal reflection, represents more of a governing oversight to maintain the structure and sustenance of those who are affiliated with that organization; both are necessary. I also noticed that apostles have the ability to pioneer and to govern, while the bishopric is largely governing in scope. Many reformations and denominations are more comfortable in using the title bishop as opposed to using the title apostle, for various reasons. Many called bishop are actually serving the kingdom as apostles. Even in accepting to serve as a bishop, I understood that I was an apostle being asked to serve in a bishop's capacity within that network.

DEACONS

"Now in those days, when the number of the disciples was multiplying, there arose a complaint against the Hebrews by the Hellenists because their widows were neglected in the daily distribution. Then the twelve summoned the multitude of the disciples and said, "It is not desirable that we should leave the word of God and serve tables. Therefore, brethren, seek out from among you seven men of good reputation, full of the Holy Spirit and wisdom, whom we may appoint over this business; but we will give ourselves continually to prayer and to the ministry of

the word." And the saying pleased the whole multitude. And they chose Stephen, a man full of faith and the Holy Spirit, and Philip, Prochorus, Nicanor, Timon, Parmenas, and Nicolas, a proselyte from Antioch, whom they set before the apostles; and when they had prayed, they laid hands on them. Then the word of God spread, and the number of the disciples multiplied greatly in Jerusalem, and a great many of the priests were obedient to the faith."

Acts 6:1-7

The disciples are addressing an issue between the Grecians and the Hebrews. The Grecians were complaining because their widows were neglected in the daily distribution and serving of food. The Twelve Disciples, now Apostles, summoned the group of disciples together to discuss the matter. They knew that the situation had to be handled, but if they were to personally attend to this, they would be pulled away for their primary commitment of prayer and the ministering of the Word.

It was not desirable for the Apostles to leave the Word to solve this pervasive problem. A more desirable and strategic way to deal with the issue was to find others that could devote their time to address the concerns while they, the Apostles, continued in the Word. From the multitude of disciples, seven men filled with the Holy Ghost and wisdom were chosen to take care of these issues. They assigned these seven to deal with the crisis, so that the Apostles could attend to continual prayer and ministry. The misconception of the phrase *"we may appoint over this business"* has resulted in thinking that deacons are over the "business" of controlling and oversight of the church, including being the pastor's supervisor or boss. When in actuality *"over the business"* pertains to the operation or service of the daily distribution of food to ensure that both the Grecian and Hebrew widows were being served and that no one was being neglected.

Deacon (or *diakonos*) is a standard ancient Greek word meaning "servant", "waiting-man", "minister", or "messenger". The ministry or service of deacons is a vital helps ministry in every church. It entails two aspects of service. First, it frees and releases pastors to commit to prayer and the ministry of the Word faithfully and diligently, which includes the studying and the preparation of the Word. Most people have no idea of the timeframe it takes for a pastor to prepare for one sermon. Personally, 20-30 hours a week has been my norm. Some may spend even more time preparing. It varies from person-to-person; however, many of my personal ministerial colleagues have shared with me that they regularly invest from 15- 30 hours on average. That is for just one sermon. Some have multiple services per weekend and preach different sermons at each service. Now consider pastors who are bi-vocational, not to mention the other weekly duties that pastors have to fulfill along with attending meetings and functions. It is extremely challenging for a pastor to effectively serve every aspect of ministry each week by himself or herself.

In recent years, we have seen an alarming rate of burnout, divorces, premature death, and suicides among pastors. There are many factors leading to these tragic statistics. We must create healthier models of pastoring. That is one reason the help ministry is so vital. Pastoral care must be extended to creating systems internally where the support and care of the pastor and family is activated. This includes, but is not limited to, vacation time, mental health counseling, and established, known boundaries where days and hours during the week are given solely for personal and family time. Other professions have a back up system to support them during their time off. Not only is it unrealistic to expect pastors and leaders to be available 24 hours a day, 7 days a week, but it is extremely unhealthy and unfair to place that demand on anyone. Healthy structures will facilitate the support needed for this to occur, plus teaching and understanding must take place in the larger body so that no one is neglected during their time of need. Still, there will be times when dire emergencies arise that require the personal attention of the pastor, but that should the exception, not the rule.

Normally, "pastoral care" as a term was used when addressing the care provided from pastors and representative persons. This care consisted of helping acts directed towards the healing, sustaining, guiding, and nurturing of persons in need. In most contexts, it is logistically unfeasible for one person to adequately serve the needs of every individual within the congregation. Therefore, secondarily, deacons are to attend to the needs of the congregation through pastoral care, so that there is no neglect within that local body. Deacons must be trained and equipped to serve basic needs such as, but not limited to, visiting others and supporting individuals who are going through challenges or losses within their lives. Their service is to be a compassionate presence offering comfort and support. When deacons visit, they are not substituting for pastors, rather they are representing the pastor and the church. Pastors should not totally abrogate visitational duties within their ministries, especially with those who are receiving end of life care or who are dealing with traumatic life altering events.

Corporately, we all must see to it that there is no neglect in the congregation. Supporting the leader requires doing your part in executing the vision so that needs are addressed and met within the local church body. In addition, it enables the ministry to reach beyond its walls and aid in serving the larger community. The mission of the church has always been to *"Go into all nations"*. The purpose of receiving the Holy Spirit, according to Acts is,

"But you shall receive power when the Holy Spirit has come upon you; and you shall be witnesses to Me in Jerusalem, and in all Judea and Samaria, and to the end of the earth."

Acts 1:8

UNDERGIRD THE VISION

"When they had taken it on board, they used cables to undergird the ship; and fearing lest they should run aground on the Syrtis Sands, they struck sail and so were driven."

Acts 27:17

Here we see a ship being tossed by a storm. The ship had been undergirded using cables and ropes, in other words, helps. The cable under the ship literally held it together in the midst of storms so that it could remain steady. The cables under the ship, though not visible, were instrumental in enduring the storm. Similarly, people supporting in the ministries of helps are not always visible. Many are working behind the scenes. The nature of helps depends on the calling for which one is anointed; however, the helps are vital to the success of the ministry. They provide administrative, governmental, spiritual, and natural support that is crucial to the health and operational aspects of any ministry or business. They also hold the ship together in the turbulent times that all ministries will go through, by keeping it stable.

When you are connected to a vision, it is important that you embrace the Horse Gate: that of providing support. Connect to the vision and be prepared to undergird it even though you may not receive a title, recognition, or honor. Do not look for a prominent seat, but undergird the ship. After all, you are doing it for the glory of God. The ministry of helps is not about big titles, big positions, or high and lofty visibility, but it is all about undergirding the ministry.

GOVERNING THE HOUSE

Concerning governmental helps, Paul states in I Corinthians, *"And God has appointed these in the church, first apostles… helps, administrations…"*

I Corinthians 12:28

Apostolic government provides direction and navigates the

ship. It gives insight concerning when to turn left, right, or when to stand still. It is the anchor that grounds the vision during adversities and storms.

"Where there is no vision, the people perish..."

Proverbs 29:18 KJV

Proper government focuses on the activity of the ministry. It sees and perceives what is taking place. It directs spiritual traffic to avoid spiritual shipwreck. It senses the urgency to give the spiritual support and strength needed to overcome storms of opposition and spiritual resistance.

"And Moses said unto Joshua, Choose us out men, and go out, fight with Amalek: tomorrow I will stand on the top of the hill with the rod of God in mine hand. So Joshua did as Moses had said to him, and fought with Amalek: and Moses, Aaron, and Hur went up to the top of the hill. And it came to pass, when Moses held up his hand, that Israel prevailed: and when he let down his hand, Amalek prevailed. But Moses' hands were heavy; and they took a stone, and put it under him, and he sat thereon; and Aaron and Hur stayed up his hands, the one on the one side, and the other on the other side; and his hands were steady until the going down of the sun. And Joshua discomfited Amalek and his people with the edge of the sword."

Exodus 17:9-13

Every vision, whether large or small, needs help. It is not good to have a visionary alone with no help. There is a connection between helps and governments. One illustration of this is found in the scripture above. Amalek fought with Israel at Rephidim. Moses instructed Joshua to choose developed and matured men to go out to fight. Never enter a spiritual battle with an infant. Instead, take the mature individuals. Moses stood on top of the hill with the rod of God in his hand. The Word further says Joshua did as Moses said, due to a trust-based relationship. As Moses released the vision, Joshua began to execute it. Joshua had received Moses' spirit and did not need to rationalize or overanalyze Moses' decisions. There must be collaboration in ministry and in other areas of our lives. For instance, in the workplace, when a supervisor gives instructions or directives to an employee, it is expected that the directive will be carried out to the best of their ability. Excellent leadership will study matters and engage in dialogue as needed, however, when decisions come down from a supervisor, it is expected to be carried out. Giving directives should be reserved for designated and special times. Those that you lead should be developed and mature in carrying out their responsibilities without micromanagement. Nevertheless, there are times in any vision when directives are required.

Insubordination is defined as defiance of authority. In most cases when this occurs, there has been some heart issues that have taken place, as well as some boundaries that have been crossed, whether verbalized or not. When one finds it challenging to follow leadership, it is time for that person to make a decision; either submit or graciously find another place of ministry or employment that is better suited to your vision/style of desired leadership. This course of action is preferred over thinking it is your assignment to straighten out leadership. Simply stated, for whatever reason, if one cannot submit to the delegated leaders and leadership structure, it is wise to find a place where you are freely able to trust and to submit, so that order can flow freely.

Look at Joshua; he did exactly what Moses asked him to do. The scripture goes on to tell us that as long as Moses' hands were up, Israel prevailed; however, whenever his hands were down, Amalek prevailed. During the battle, Moses' hands became tired from being lifted and extended for such a lengthy period, then the ministry of helps and government appeared. Aaron, representing government, and Hur, representing helps, had Moses sit on a stone and the two of them held up his hands until the going down of the sun. Because of the support of Aaron and Hur, Joshua defeated Amalek and his people with the edge of his sword.

Everyone is needed in ministry. Peoples' presence and gifts are of great support to fully execute the assignment given to visionaries. The assignment for Aaron and Hur was to undergird Moses' hands when they became too heavy for him to continue to hold up on his own. Similarly, you are called to undergird your spiritual leader in holding up their hands in the ministry.

SUPPORT STRENGTH

As mentioned earlier, the Horse Gate deals with the strength and the ability to support and carry the load or the vision. Man, in his natural ability, can carry a load.

Biblically, when the load is too heavy for men, horses were

utilized. Help is necessary to fulfill the vision when the load is too heavy to carry. It is at the Horse Gate where individuals receive the strength to carry out weighty assignments. It is self-defeating to place some weighty responsibilities upon those who are not reliable and dependable. Maturity speaks of an individual's strength to carry loads without them becoming fragile and weakened by the various challenges of life and ministry. Appointing weak, immature, or undeveloped individuals to weighty tasks could be destructive to them personally as well as to the entire vision.

HEART AND SPEED OF SUPPORTERS

"So the Lord said to Moses: "Gather to Me seventy men of the elders of Israel, whom you know to be the elders of the people and officers over them; bring them to the tabernacle of meeting, that they may stand there with you. Then I will come down and talk with you there. I will take of the Spirit that is upon you and will put the same upon them; and they shall bear the burden of the people with you, that you may not bear it yourself alone."

Numbers 11:16-17

It is necessary to receive the spirit of the leader. God never intended for Moses to carry the vision alone, but to share it with those who had the same spirit as Moses. Those who are serving in leadership must have the spirit of their leader in order to properly execute the assignment.

At the Horse Gate, we learn to be swift and agile; possessing the ability to carry the vision for a longer distance. The difference between a horse and a mule is not the strength to carry, but the swiftness with which it moves. You cannot train a mule, as it is stubborn; but a horse is swift, agile, and highly trainable. The Horse Gate not only deals with the strength and endurance, but also the ability to be trained to carry the vision for the long haul.

SUPPORT: LOYALTY

Loyalty is unwavering allegiance. It is rooted in faith that binds two hearts together in covenant.

"Now when he had finished speaking to Saul, the soul of Jonathan was knit to the soul of David, and Jonathan loved him as his own soul. Saul took him that day and would not let him go home to his father's house anymore. Then Jonathan and David made a covenant, because he loved him as his own soul. And Jonathan took off the robe that was on him and gave it to David, with his armor, even to his sword and his bow and his belt."

I Samuel 18:1-4

David and Jonathan are an example of the anointing of loyalty. Jonathan loved David as his own soul. His spirit was knitted to David although he knew David was anointed to be the next king. Jonathan understood and accepted the fact that David would be the one to succeed Saul, although he, Jonathan, was Saul's son and rightful heir. As a symbol of his loyalty, Jonathan stripped off his robe and gave it to David. David accepted it as a covenant of loyalty. In addition to giving David his royal robe, Jonathan also gave him his sword, bow and girdle.

This type of loyalty is rarely seen these days, even in the House of God. Loyalty is an essential anointing needed for the long haul. Loyalty is not always convenient, yet it is unwavering, even in the midst of challenging times. Its essence is that you will always commit to doing the honorable things to better the other person, even when it requires you to make personal sacrifices.

SUPPORT: PURPOSE

> *"Jesus said unto them, my meat is to do the will of him that sent me, and to finish his work."*
>
> *John 4:34 KJV*

The Son of God came to this earth with a divine purpose. He was sent to do the will of His Father. He lived a sinless life, died on the cross for our sins, and was resurrected on the third day so that He could be manifested and destroy the work of the devil. The loyalty of David and Jonathan fulfilled a divine assignment as well. Undergird the vision until the end with the anointing of purpose.

SUPPORT: FINISHING

A horse can carry a weighty load even after it has been aged and weakened by time. It does this by employing the finishing anointing. Sometimes it will be hard on you to carry the load, but during those times, we must seek God for His grace to enable us to complete the tasks. Carrying any load is a challenge in-and-of itself; however, it becomes significantly more severe during times of ministry or personal turbulence. One must remain focused and not get sidetracked.

"I have glorified You on the earth. I have finished the work which You have given Me to do."

John 17:4

"I have fought the good fight, I have finished the race, I have kept the faith."

II Timothy 4:7

Jesus fulfilled His purpose on earth with this finishing anointing. Endurance is necessary to be a good soldier for Christ. You must fight until the end and fight to win the battle.

"Looking unto Jesus the author and the finisher of our faith; who for the joy that was set before him endured the cross, despising the shame, and is set down at the right hand of the throne of God."

Hebrews 12:2

Neither the swift nor the strong wins the race, but the one who endures to the end wins. Whatever you do for His Kingdom is not in vain. Jesus Christ endured the cross for the joy that was set before Him, and is now seated at the right hand of the throne of God. No matter what the circumstances are that you are facing,

He is right there to help you. You might find yourself slowing down, but do not quit. Keep persevering.

> *"I commend to you Phoebe our sister, who is a servant of the church in Cenchrea, that you may receive her in the Lord in a manner worthy of the saints, and assist her in whatever business she has need of you; for indeed she has been a helper of many and of myself also. Greet Priscilla and Aquila, my fellow workers in Christ Jesus, who risked their own necks for my life, to whom not only I give thanks, but also all the churches of the Gentiles."*
>
> *Romans 16:1-4*

Paul tells the Romans to assist Phoebe, their sister in Christ, for she was of major help to them in their ministry. Priscilla and Aquila were also his helpers. They were ready to lay down their lives for the sake of Paul and his ministry. These women were phenomenal supporters of Paul's ministry. Always position yourself to capture the heart of the visionaries you are assigned to, as well as those who are assigned to your vision.

CHAPTER 9

THE PLACE OF REVELATION

"After them Zadok the son of Immer made repairs in front of his own house. After him Shemaiah the son of Shechaniah, the keeper of the East Gate, made repairs."

Nehemiah 3:29

The East Gate represents new beginnings, the beginning of a new day, the beginning of new opportunities, and the beginning of a new and glorious vision. Of all the gates mentioned in the book of Nehemiah, the East Gate was the gate that opened first each day. Each new day begins with the sun rising in the east. The relationship between the rising of the sun and the East Gate is that, symbolically, they both deal with a fresh revelation. Each new day dispels the darkness and releases a new light or new revelation.

It is the will of God for apostolic centers to be used to literally blast the kingdom of darkness. You cannot blast the kingdom of darkness with ignorance. You cannot blast it with traditions.

You cannot blast it with ritual. The only thing that can blast the kingdom of darkness is the power of the Word of God. It will be accomplished through vessels of God who are filled with His Word and impregnated with the revelation and the anointing to go into the kingdom of darkness.

"Then he brought me back to the door of the temple; and there was water, flowing from under the threshold of the temple toward the east, for the front of the temple faced east; the water was flowing from under the right side of the temple, south of the altar. He brought me out by way of the north gate and led me around on the outside to the outer gateway that faces east; and there was water, running out on the right side.

And when the man went out to the east with the line in his hand, he measured one thousand cubits, and he brought me through the waters; the water came up to my ankles. Again, he measured one thousand and brought me through the waters; the water came up to my knees. Again, he measured one thousand and brought me through; the water came up to my waist. Again he measured one thousand, and it was a river that I could not cross; for the water was too deep, water in which one must swim, a river that could not be crossed."

Ezekiel 47:1-5

Look at what is happening here in the Word of God. First, the waters were ankle deep. As we read further, the waters became knee deep, but it does not stop there - the scripture says the waters rose to the loins. Finally, the waters become so deep that Ezekiel could not pass over or through them. The waters were high over and above his head. Symbolically, this shows a progression of revelation. Notice that the water is released from the House of God. It issues out from under the threshold eastward.

The description of what we see taking place, beginning with the ankle-deep water, symbolizes there is more of your will in the waters than God's. This means that God is only in control of a small portion of your life. In ankle deep water, you are walking by your own strength and ability. You are able to move in and out freely like a child playing in water. Because of the depth of the water (anointing) you are in, you are only able to tap into the shallow things of God. You are not able to tap into deeper streams of revelation knowledge because you are still spiritually immature.

Shifting from ankle deep to knee deep, reflects an increase of revelation. We see the increase, as water at the knee level is symbolic of submission to God. We bow down on our knees as a sign of surrendering our will and seeking His will. At the knee level, this level of anointing causes us to develop a prayer life. We have been sanctioned by God's Spirit to enter into a place of intimacy with the Father. Producing a greater level of sensitivity as we yield in His presence, offering our prayers unto Him as He speaks and sharpens our ears to discern His voice.

Many will stay in ankle deep water and not progress to this deeper place of intimacy. It is possible to know and to recite His Word, yet due to prayerlessness there is no anointing on our lives. They are not yet at the point of surrendering their will for His will. God desires for us not to remain stagnant in ankle deep water, but to be able to progress into deeper waters.

The next level of water rises to the loins. This is the place of reproduction, increase, and multiplication. Because you have allowed the Word of God to take root in your heart and have developed a prayer life with Him, you are now able to reproduce. You are no longer operating in the flesh and seeking self-gratification. You are focused on being fruitful and multiplying. Not only do you yield more fruitfulness in your character (*Galatians 5* – the fruit of the Spirit), but you begin to reproduce other believers through new birth and discipling.

Finally, in verse five, the water is so deep that Ezekiel could not pass over. This deals with being filled, saturated, and absorbed by the presence of the Holy Ghost. At this level, the Word of God is releasing new dimensional revelation into your life with such force, that you cannot even fight against it. All you can do is receive because it is above your head. You cannot comprehend this level of revelation and insight that God has for your life. It is far beyond natural ability. At this point, you are no longer trying to figure out what God is doing, you just go with the flow and do as He leads you in the Spirit. Your maturation is now manifesting and being released. The aim and goal of this process is total immersion in Him. Symbolically, it starts at the ankle, moves to the knee, then to the loins and lastly, up and over the head.

"For as many as are led by the Spirit of God, they are the sons of God."

Romans 8:14

The prophet Ezekiel lets us know that it takes water to produce life. He prophesied that wherever the water goes, they shall live. Because these waters come and bring life, there shall be a great multitude of fish. These waters shall bring healing and produce life.

"And it shall be that every living thing that moves, wherever the rivers go, will live. There will be a very great multitude of fish, because these waters go there; for they will be healed, and everything will live wherever the river goes."

Ezekiel 47:9

"Then Jesus said to them, 'Follow Me, and I will make you become fishers of men.'"

Mark 1:17

All of this relates back to the East gate as it deals with the release of water, which is revelation. The ending of this scripture says everything shall live wherever the water comes. In other words, according to the book of Proverbs, *"Where there is no vision, the people perish"*. Another translation says, *"Where there is no redemptive revelation the people perish"*. It is not what you know in your head that is going to keep you alive, rather it is what you know in your spirit. Head knowledge is useless when you are confronting the enemy. The spirit of man is the candle of the Lord.

"That the God of our Lord Jesus Christ, the Father of glory, may give to you the spirit of wisdom and revelation in the knowledge of Him, the eyes of your understanding being enlightened; that

you may know what is the hope of His calling, what are the
riches of the glory of His inheritance in the saints,"

Ephesians 1:17-18

We need revelation knowledge to open our eyes in order to
have total victory over the enemy and his devices. Revelation lifts
us to a higher level in every area of our lives. The Lord says to
Nicodemus, *"Except a man be born again, he cannot see the kingdom
of God."* Like Nicodemus, we were made to operate on a higher
plane than just head knowledge. We were created to live by revelation in our heart. The Word says in I Peter

"...who called you out of darkness into His marvelous light;"

I Peter 2:9

Revelation knowledge brings light where darkness once existed. The dawning of each new day and new season begins at the
East Gate.

*"That the God of our Lord Jesus Christ, the Father of glory, may
give to you the spirit of wisdom and revelation in the knowledge
of Him,"*

Ephesians 1:17

The wisdom and revelation referred to above is obtained at the
East Gate. With the insight and the revelation that God gives
us, we have the ability to do warfare in dark arenas. You cannot
defeat the schemes of the enemy using your intellect because
there are many demons educationally smarter than you are. Head
knowledge is rendered null and void in the Spirit realm; however,

we can tap into the revelation knowledge that He reveals to us. When we operate in the arena of knowledge, we make the enemy mad and defeat him on every side. Regardless of strongholds in the region, in the city, or in our families, when the East Gate is opened in your life, the power of God will come in and dispel all forms of darkness.

Some people will not understand that the wisdom and revelation that flows from the East Gate can produce great growth. Many try to understand this with their natural eye and natural mind. Because they are spiritually blinded, they cannot see or understand it through spiritual sight and comprehension. They are leaning on their own understanding using their head knowledge. Clearly, the Word of God admonishes us to not lean to our own understanding (*Proverbs 3:5*). If we lean to our understanding, then we will never understand the move of God. It will never make any sense to us because His thoughts are not our thoughts and His ways are not our ways. Solomon reminds us that,

"The spirit of a man is the lamp of the Lord..."
Proverbs 20:27

Revelation occurs when the lamp or candle of the Lord enlightens our spirit.

At the East Gate, God releases insight. He opens a spiritual dimension and allows your insight to see and receive it. He provides direction for you. He gives you everything you need pertaining to life and godliness for each new day. If you are faithful to His Word and live His Word, when you dwell at the East Gate, fresh revelation is released to you that will propel you to another level in Him. God is raising up apostolic centers that flow in revelation, but if you continue to operate only in familiar ways, you are going to miss it. If you continue to do what you have always done, then expect to get what you have always gotten. However, if you want to walk in newness and receive fresh anointing and fresh revelation, then you must get in the water.

The East Gate does not only deal with the influx of revelation, but the prophetic significance of the East Gate also deals with two things: The coming of the glory of the Lord and the coming of the Lord of glory.

THE COMING OF THE GLORY

"Afterward he brought me to the gate, the gate that faces toward the east. And behold, the glory of the God of Israel came from the way of the east. His voice was like the sound of many waters; and the earth shone with His glory."

Ezekiel 43:1-2

The first prophetic significance of the East Gate for the people of Israel deals with the coming of the Glory of the Lord. According to the Word of God, the glory comes from the way of the east. This lets us know that if there is no East Gate, then there is no glory coming. Without revelation, there will never be glory. What Moses was really saying when he said to God, *"Show us your glory"*; was "show me the revelation of who you are". God's glory comes in where there is revelation. If there is no revelation, there will be no glory.

"And the glory of the Lord came into the temple by way of the gate which faces toward the east. The Spirit lifted me up and brought me into the inner court; and behold, the glory of the Lord filled the temple."

Ezekiel 43:4-5

THE LORD OF GLORY

"For as the lightning comes from the east and flashes to the west, so also will the coming of the Son of Man be."

Matthew 24:27

Secondly, the East Gate deals with the coming of the Lord of Glory. Just as the lightning comes out of the east, God said that His Son will be coming back and making His appearance in the same manner. He is coming from the east.

"The earth is the Lord's, and all its fullness, The world and those who dwell therein. For He has founded it upon the seas, And established it upon the waters.

Who may ascend into the hill of the Lord? Or who may stand in His holy place? He who has clean hands and a pure heart, Who has not lifted up his soul to an idol, Nor sworn deceitfully. He shall receive blessing from the Lord, And righteousness from the God of his salvation. This is Jacob, the generation of those who seek Him, Who seek Your face. Selah

Lift up your heads, O you gates! And be lifted up, you everlasting doors! And the King of glory shall come in. Who is this King of glory? The Lord strong and mighty, The Lord mighty in battle. Lift up your heads, O you gates! Lift up, you everlasting doors! And the King of glory shall come in. Who is this King of glory? The Lord of hosts, He is the King of glory. Selah"

Psalm 24:1-10

Prophetically, this Psalm is dealing with the second coming of the Lord Jesus Christ. *Psalm 24:7* speaks of the King of Glory coming in. The East Gate is the gate out of which God's glory is coming back. The second coming of the Lord Jesus Christ will be out of the East Gate.

He is coming back, and we need to live like we know He is coming back. We need to testify like we know He is coming back. He is coming back. God's desire is that none should perish. Even though we know some will, He is still depending on you and me to spread the good news of His return.

He wants us to share with others the insight that He releases to us at the East Gate. We are mandated to share it because people are perishing for lack of knowledge. Releasing the revelation knowledge of His return is going to set the atmosphere for His return in a strong and mighty way.

CHAPTER 10

The Gate Miphkad

THE PLACE OF ASSIGNMENT

"After him Malchijah, one of the goldsmiths, made repairs as far as the house of the Nethinim and of the merchants, in front of the Miphkad Gate, and as far as the upper room at the corner."

Nehemiah 3:31

The Gate of Miphkad reveals the importance and significance of the assignment. This is where your assignment is realized and birthed. At the Gate of Miphkad, not only is your assignment realized, but also God's preordained timing for your appointed place is also given there. Many people are not on their assignments; therefore, they miss their appointment.

You have to be connected with the Spirit of the Lord so that you recognize your assigned and appointed place. God is not going to give you an exemption because you were out of place. He is going to hold you accountable. It is up to you to ensure that you are in the will of God. God is always ready to speak to you, but if you are not in your appointed place, you will not hear what God is saying concerning the assignment over your life.

The Gate of Miphkad deals with the assignment and the appointed place. It is also referred to as the Inspection Gate. It is important that the apostolic center and people represent excellence in how assignments are carried out. God is not only concerned with you performing the assignment and being on point, but He is ultimately concerned with your heart as it pertains to the matter. The way in which you show up for the appointment and perform the assignment determines if you are a son or a servant.

SERVANT OR SON

"..."Well done, good and faithful servant;..."

Matthew 25:21

"..."This is my beloved Son, in whom I am well pleased.""

Matthew 3:17

There are two very different and very distinct responses given to the servant and to the son. To the servant He says, "well done", but of His son He says, "I am well pleased." You may have carried out your task and performed it well, but just because you performed it well does not mean that it has pleased God. When you do something with the wrong attitude, disposition, or motive, even if you have done it well, it will not be pleasing unto the Father. You have done it as a servant, not as a child unto the Lord. Those that take pleasure in completing an assignment are those that God refers to as His children. Those that do not murmur and complain in the process of the assignment. The heart of completing an assignment is what sets the servant apart from the son. The spirit makes the difference.

Servants are solely concerned with completing the task and are not concerned about bringing honor or pleasure to the Father. They are simply task driven. Those who understand that they represent the heart of God are committed to bringing pleasure to the Father while doing the task. As we focus on pleasing God, He begins to release more of His glory over our lives. He becomes confident in us and knows that we are not going to misuse His glory. He trusts us and knows that we are going to continue in our assignment for His glory.

Mature children do not take the blessings of God for granted. Appointed servants may take the master's goodness and kindness for granted; subsequently they may be serving only for what He gives and what is due them. Appointed sons serve because they have come to know that a loving and kind Father has blessed them. They willingly serve with a heart of gratitude. It is their reasonable service to do so, for the service they render gives their Father honor.

So again, the Gate of Miphkad deals with the appointed place because that is where your assignment is. It is also worth mentioning again that the Gate of Miphkad deals with inspection and judgment. God not only wants to know if you are doing the assignment, but He also wants to know how you are doing it. He is looking at your motive for doing what has been assigned and

He is looking to see if there is a hidden agenda.

THE JUDGMENT SEAT OF CHRIST

At the Gate of Miphkad, we are dealing with two judgments. The first judgment deals with the judgment seat of Christ. This refers to the judgment for believers.

"For we must all appear before the judgment seat of Christ, that each one may receive the things done in the body, according to what he has done, whether good or bad."

II Corinthians 5:10

As believers, our works will be tried and judged. He will examine your heart. You are going to appear before the judgment seat of Christ and receive judgment for the things you have done, whether good or bad.

God has a word for the unbeliever as well because we will all be judged. It does not matter that someone does not believe in God or the Word of God, because on judgment day they will all have to give account for their unbelief. Because they do not believe, they may live their life as if there really is no God, as if they will not have to give an account for any of their actions. Regardless, judgment will come.

THE GREAT WHITE THRONE JUDGMENT

The Great White Throne Judgment is where unbelievers who

have denied the name of Christ and have not accepted Him as their Lord and Savior will face the Holy God. This is where the judgment of the unbeliever will take place.

The unbeliever will not be judged solely for the work they have or have not done, but they will be judged for not accepting the Son of God. It is at the Great White Throne that the unbeliever will have to give an account for denying the finished work of Calvary's redeemer, the work of His only begotten Son. The Word of God says,

"The fool hath said in his heart, there is no God..."

Psalm 14:1

BELIEVER'S CROWN

"Finally, there is laid up for me the crown of righteousness, which the Lord, the righteous Judge, will give to me on that Day, and not to me only but also to all who have loved His appearing."

II Timothy 4:8

As a believer, you are on assignment and the Lord has reserved for you crowns or rewards that will let you know that He is well pleased with your service unto Him. The first crown is the crown of righteousness that will be given to all of those who have loved his appearing.

"And everyone who competes for the prize is temperate in all

things. Now they do it to obtain a perishable crown, but we for an imperishable crown."

I Corinthians 9:25

Then we see the incorruptible crown, given to those who strive for mastery and for excellence. As a believer, you are not called to be average or a part of the crowd. You must be willing to move beyond normalcy and operate in excellence. The Bible says that Daniel had an excellent spirit in him. Paul instructs us that whatever you do, do it heartily, as to the Lord and not to men (*Colossians 3:23*). Saints, remember whom you are serving and strive to serve Him daily with excellence and mastery.

"For what is our hope, or joy, or crown of rejoicing? Is it not even you in the presence of our Lord Jesus Christ at His coming? For you are our glory and joy."

I Thessalonians 2:19-20

The third crown lifted up in the Word is the crown of rejoicing, also called the soul winner's crown. The mission of apostolic centers is to make disciples of all nations. We are called to aid people in their personal relationship with the Lord. We accomplish this mission by establishing local ministries and through evangelism and missions. Salvation is the priority.

"And when the Chief Shepherd appears, you will receive the crown of glory that does not fade away."

I Peter 5:4

The fourth crown is the crown of glory. This crown is also known as the Shepherd's Crown. The Word of the Lord says in Jeremiah,

> *"And I will give you shepherds according to My heart, who will feed you with knowledge and understanding."*
>
> *Jeremiah 3:15*

Do you know that pastors are gifts from God? Pastors represent the heart of God and according to I Peter 5:1-4, their ministry is to feed the sheep with knowledge (revelation) and understanding and to lead the flock in accordance with Acts 20:28.

> *"Do not fear any of those things which you are about to suffer. Indeed, the devil is about to throw some of you into prison, that you may be tested, and you will have tribulation ten days. Be faithful until death, and I will give you the crown of life."*
>
> *Revelation 2:10*

The last crown is the crown of life, also referred to as the martyr's crown. This crown is given to those who have endured and have been victorious over trials and persecution, even to the point of death. In the beatitudes Jesus said, *"Blessed are those who are persecuted for righteousness' sake for theirs is the Kingdom of Heaven."* *(Matthew 5)*. Paul admonishes us, *"if we suffer, we shall also reign with him"* *(II Timothy 2:12)*.

SUPPORTING YOUR PASTOR

It is pivotal that individuals understand the importance of

providing support to pastors. Pastors have been given the charge to oversee the flock through feeding them the Word of God and by guarding them against harm (Acts 28:20).

Here are a few ways that individuals can support their pastors:

With Your Prayers

"Therefore I exhort first of all that supplications, prayers, intercessions, and giving of thanks be made for all men, for kings and all who are in authority, that we may lead a quiet and peaceable life in all godliness and reverence."

I Timothy 2:1-2

We all expect pastors to pray for those they lead; however, it is just as important that individuals pray continuously for their pastors and family. The enemy fully understands the impact of attacking the head and the subsequent effect it has on the body (Zechariah 13:7). Pray for protection, wisdom, health, and prosperity as they lead the flock as well as praying for their individual family members.

With Your Words

"Death and life are in the power of the tongue,..."

Proverbs 18:21

As pastors continuously encourage the flock with their words, one great way to support your pastor is with words of encouragement. Just as Caleb encouraged Moses by quieting the people who were talking negatively, he also brought great encouragement to him by saying that they (the children of Israel) are well able to take possession of the land and to overcome the enemy (Numbers 13:30). Unfortunately, many have been discouraged in pastoral leadership due to the vocal minority getting most of the attention. The colloquial expression that "the squeaky wheel gets grease" is far too often the case. One of the most famous quotes by Dr. Martin L. King is so applicable, "In the end, we will remember not the words of our enemies, but the silence of our friends."

With Honor

"Let the elders who rule well be counted worthy of double honor, especially those who labor in the word and doctrine. For the Scripture says, "You shall not muzzle an ox while it treads out the grain," and, "The laborer is worthy of his wages."

I Timothy 5:17-18

Honor is the highest level of respect and admiration one person can have for another. To hold your pastor in high esteem is extremely important. You can only receive from those you honor. Even in the midst of a disagreement, honor must be paramount. One's loyalty is in direct proportion to the level of honor you have for your leader. It is impossible to be disloyal to your leader if you honor them.

Paul also understood that honor is reflected in the degree to which you sow into their lives, enabling them to be free financially. One of the greatest weights upon pastoral leadership is being restricted financially. It inhibits the ability to freely minister when pastors are strained and stretched thin due to financial weights upon the ministry and upon their personal lives.

CHAPTER 11

The Gate of Ephraim

THE PLACE OF FRUIT AND HARVEST

"And from above the gate of Ephraim…"

Nehemiah 12:39

We are now entering the Gate of Ephraim. Ephraim literally means doubly blessed, doubly fruitful, or fruitfulness.

"And the name of the second he called Ephraim: For God has caused me to be fruitful in the land of my affliction."

Genesis 41:52

Ephraim was the name of Joseph's second son. He was given that name to symbolize the fruitfulness of his father. Similarly, apostolic centers are characterized by their fruitfulness.

The scripture says Joseph was fruitful in the land of his affliction. Later, this anointing and blessing was passed to his son Ephraim as a double portion and fruitful anointing.

THE FRUITFUL BOUGH

"But his father refused and said, "I know, my son, I know. He also shall become a people, and he also shall be great; but truly his younger brother shall be greater than he, and his descendants shall become a multitude of nations."

Genesis 48:19

In this scripture, we find Israel (Jacob) blessing Manasseh and Ephraim, the Egyptian- born sons of Joseph. Ephraim, the youngest, is given the blessing that was traditionally reserved for the oldest, Manasseh. Jacob gives this blessing to Ephraim at the displeasure of their father Joseph, but in accordance with the divine will of God. Ephraim's blessing was the double portion blessing, normally reserved for the eldest son. Later, Moses also recognizes and blesses Ephraim to be doubly fruitful by stating,

"... They are the ten thousands of Ephraim, And they are the thousands of Manasseh."

Deuteronomy 33:17

Ephraim would and had become greater than his brother Manasseh. Ephraim was doubly blessed and fruitful.

Another example of this double portion or doubly fruitful anointing is Elisha, Elijah's spiritual son. He received the double portion mantle of Elijah. It is noteworthy to mention the miracles that he performed far surpassed those of Elijah.

As believers, the Gate of Ephraim symbolizes God's intention toward humankind from the beginning of creation, to be fruitful and blessed. Fruitfulness is a sign of answered prayers.

"Then God blessed them, and God said to them, 'Be fruitful and multiply; fill the earth and subdue it; have dominion over the fish of the sea, over the birds of the air, and over every living thing that moves on the earth.'"

Genesis 1:28

The five-fold charge is given in *Genesis 1:28*. The first charge is to be fruitful. In other words, we are instructed to be productive. As fertile, creative beings, we are called to produce in the earth. God has placed in us, from the beginning, the ability to produce. God would never charge us or command us to do a thing that He has not graced and equipped us to perform. Secondly, the charge is to multiply or increase ourselves through reproduction. God commands us to be fruitful and duplicate ourselves. Thirdly, we are charged to replenish the earth. That means we are to refill or add to the earth.

Job states the plain universal truth of our lives, *"Naked came I out of my mother's womb and naked shall I return thither."* Here, Job is stating the simple fact that we have brought nothing into the world and we will take nothing with us when we depart. Perhaps this means our sole purpose for being here is to add to and bring increase to the earth realm. We were created to bless the Lord.

The fourth charge is to subdue the earth, which means to bring it under control and under our dominion. God has charged us to bring creation under our control. The last and final charge is to have dominion or "to have kingdom" in the earth. We cannot pick or choose from these charges. It is the will of God that we implement all five of the charges. These charges given to us are to empower us for the implementation of kingdom dominion in the earth realm.

TAKE THE LIMITS OFF

"I am the true vine, and My Father is the vinedresser. Every branch in Me that does not bear fruit He takes away; and every branch that bears fruit He prunes, that it may bear more fruit."

John 15:1-2

At the Gate of Ephraim, we deal with being fruitful. That speaks of quantity and quality. God commands us to be fruitful and multiply. Our lives have to be committed to continuous growth. As we become more rooted and grounded in our relationship with our heavenly Father, we progress in our ability to produce fruit. That is one sign of a healthy relationship with Him.

God purges and prunes fruit bearing branches, just like a gardener, in order for them to bring forth more fruit. Dead branches and dead leaves that are unproductive and unfruitful have to be, and should be, cut off. If you let the dead branches stay attached, they will drain the life from and kill off the living branches. The branches that are fruitful and plentifully producing will have to be purged and pruned to make room for more growth. When God does this, He is showing you He loves you enough to come to you, as the husbandman and as the gardener, to clip off and take away the dead areas of your life.

Oftentimes we are so determined to stay connected to the dead areas of our lives, those areas that are not producing, that it becomes detrimental. These attachments, whether known or unknown, are not productive to our assignment and the purging and pruning of these areas is painful because of our familiarity with them.

"You are already clean because of the word which I have spoken to you. Abide in Me, and I in you. As the branch cannot bear fruit of itself, unless it abides in the vine, neither can you, unless you abide in Me.

"I am the vine, you are the branches. He who abides in Me, and I in him, bears much fruit; for without Me you can do nothing. If anyone does not abide in Me, he is cast out as a branch and is withered; and they gather them and throw them into the fire, and they are burned. If you abide in Me, and My words abide in you, you will ask what you desire, and it shall be done for you."

John 15:3-7

Our productivity is directly dependent upon our connection with Him. Apart from Him, we are utterly unproductive. His Word must be the anchor of our lives, visions, and assignment. His Word is the thread that must be woven into the very fabric of our lives.

God desires to be glorified as He walks with you through the various challenges that you encounter. It is not His aim for you to stay in darkness, debt, or discouragement. He gets the glory when you persevere through the challenges presented, and start bearing fruit from the situations that tried to restrict you. As painful and difficult as things can become, He takes delight in seeing us trusting Him and His Word as we endeavor to manifest fruitfulness in every capacity of our lives.

"By this all will know that you are My disciples, if you have love for one another."

John 13:35

"Jesus said to him, "'You shall love the Lord your God with all your heart, with all your soul, and with all your mind.' This is the first and great commandment. And the second is like it: 'You shall love your neighbor as yourself.'"

Matt 22:37-39

"If someone says, "I love God," and hates his brother, he is a liar; for he who does not love his brother whom he has seen, how can he love God whom he has not seen? And this commandment we have from Him: that he who loves God must love his brother also."

I John 4:20-21

Fruitfulness also speaks to the increase of one's character as demonstrated through the fruit of the spirit (*Galatians 5*). So often, fruitfulness is measured by the size of one's vision as opposed to the amount of love that is exhibited in one's life. Our character represents the inner working of God's Spirit in our lives. As these fruits develop, our lives will reflect the nature and heart of God to those we are called to lead and to serve. We become the vessel that is used to display the attributes and personality of the kingdom.

Above all, the kingdom of God is represented by love. It is the greatest force within the kingdom. God's heart is not just in the reproduction and multiplication of visions, but the expansion of love. We must grow daily in our love walk towards God, self, and others. As we are intentionally focusing on the fruit of the spirit, we must intentionally display love to others. Love is strong enough to handle the differences within relationships, as well as secure enough to celebrate it. Love is not abrasive and judgmental; love is kind, love is patient.

HARVEST TIME

In addition to the Gate of Ephraim signifying fruitfulness, it also refers to or is associated with the Feast of Tabernacles. The Feast of Tabernacles is God's pattern for the last day harvest. The children of Israel came together to rebuild and restore the gates. They assembled and gathered themselves together to accomplish the work. They were thankful for the freedom from captivity and looked forward to better days to come. The Feast of the Tabernacles can be associated with the end-time harvest where we, as believers and as workers in the field, bring in the harvest for God. The field is the world in which we live now. We must stay mindful that the world is only our temporary home. We are sojourners and pilgrims, placed here to accomplish a job. We have work to do. The people of God must come to the realization and understanding that harvest time is now. It is time for all the sons and daughters that have been called and ordained by God to come forth and be birthed into the kingdom. It is time for the nations to be turned back to the Lord. It is time for the Lord and His name to be praised in all the earth. That is why it is so very important that we pray for the nations and for our families now. It is of vital importance that we intercede and petition the Lord for the release of those called to work. We pray for the release of harvesters to the fields for the end-time gathering. We have to pray that the Lord of the Harvest will send forth the laborers into their appointed and assigned fields to gather His harvest.

We cannot afford to have church as usual, because God is gathering up His last day harvest. It is time for us to come out-side the doors of the church and take the church to the streets, to the cities, and to the nations. God is looking for laborers that are willing and ready to reap souls for Him. He is looking for minis-try gifts that can be released to the marketplace for the harvesting of hearts and the souls of men.

According to the Word of God, the Gate of Ephraim signifies fruitfulness and multiplication (*Deuteronomy 33:17*). Before you can sow a seed, God says I am bringing it back to you multiplied. God says I am adding to your seed sown because My word says that if you give, I will give it back to you multiplied; thirty, sixty, and even one hundred fold. Because He knows your thoughts from afar off, before you lay your prayer requests on the altar, He says, I have already answered them. Because it is God and only God who causes us to be fruitful and He alone causes it to multiply, we can be assured that the harvest is ripe and ready for the picking. It is harvest time and God is ready to bring as many as have been called into the kingdom of the Living God!

CHAPTER 12

The Prison Gate

THE PLACE OF GUARDING THE HARVEST

"And above the Gate of Ephraim, above the Old Gate, above the Fish Gate, the Tower of Hananel, the Tower of [a]the Hundred, as far as the Sheep Gate; and they stopped by the Gate of the Prison."

Nehemiah 12:39

To understand the purpose of the Prison Gate, let us look at the Word of God.

"So He drove out the man; and He placed cherubim at the east of the garden of Eden, and a flaming sword which turned every way, to guard the way to the tree of life."

Genesis 3:24

In correlation to the Word of God, the Prison Gate is symbolic of guarding, watching, and protecting that which is holy, so that it does not become tainted or corrupted. In Genesis 3:24, the assignment of the Cherubim was to keep the holy and sacred undefiled. The disobedience of Adam and Eve corrupted the holy purpose of God and the place of their assignment in the earth. Through their disobedience, they allowed sin and corruption into the world. Because corruption had made its appearance in a consecrated and holy place, the Garden of Eden could no longer be their place of assignment. This called for immediate action on God's part to safeguard it from further corruption. God set in place a method of guarding, watching, and protecting what was holy to Him.

As in the Garden of Eden, God now shows up at the Prison Gate to do war on behalf of His chosen people. He is Jehovah Gibbor, the Mighty Man of War, who wars for righteousness' sake. He is there to protect that which is holy unto the Lord.

"The Lord is thy keeper;..."

Psalm 121:5

THE RESPONSIBILITY OF THE GATEKEEPER

The Word of God says,

"Because it is written, 'Be holy, for I am holy.'"

I Peter 1:16

By this pronouncement, God is letting us know that He considers us holy, sacred, consecrated, and set apart vessels for Himself. We are His treasures in earthen vessels. He lives and dwells within us. Accordingly, He is obligated to protect that which is holy to Him. He has obligated Himself to protect and keep us.

At the Prison Gate there are assigned guards, just like at the east of the Garden of Eden where we find the assigned Cherubim. At the Prison Gate, God does not haphazardly select and assign guard duty to just anyone. He appoints gatekeepers to this duty, just as He did the Levities and the priests. He will only appoint gatekeepers who have a reverence for the holy and sacred things of God.

Those that He appoints as gatekeepers are responsible to protect the anointing and to protect the things of God. They are appointed to keep the way of the tree of life. They are to be ready at all times to do warfare over and against anything or anyone that would come up against the holiness of God.

In *I Chronicles Chapter 9*, we find reference to Gatekeepers. They had several responsibilities:

- They were to guard the threshold.

- They were responsible for the rooms and the treasures in the house.

- They had charge of the keys to open up the temple and the tabernacle.

- They were in charge of the oracles being used. (This was very important because if anything were tainted, it would interfere with the holiness of God; therefore, it was crucial that the proper garments and instruments were being used to bring honor and worship unto the Lord.)

- They were responsible for taking care of the furnishings within the house of God.

Looking at the Prison Gate and the gatekeepers assigned to safeguard and protect the holy things of God, we can examine the life of Obed-Edom, who is a prime example of a pleasing gatekeeper.

"Again David gathered all the choice men of Israel, thirty thousand. And David arose and went with all the people who were with him from Baale Judah to bring up from there the ark of God, whose name is called by the Name, the Lord of Hosts, who dwells between the cherubim. So they set the ark of God on a new cart, and brought it out of the house of Abinadab, which was on the hill; and Uzzah and Ahio, the sons of Abinadab, drove the new cart. And they brought it out of the house of Abinadab, which was on the hill, accompanying the ark of God; and Ahio went before the ark. Then David and all the house of Israel played music before the Lord on all kinds of instruments of fir wood, on harps, on stringed instruments, on tambourines, on sistrums, and on cymbals.

And when they came to Nachon's threshing floor, Uzzah put out his hand to the ark of God and took hold of it, for the oxen stumbled. Then the anger of the Lord was aroused against Uzzah, and God struck him there for his error; and he died there by the ark of God. And David became angry because of the Lord's outbreak against Uzzah; and he called the name of the place Perez

Uzzah to this day.

David was afraid of the Lord that day; and he said, "How can the ark of the Lord come to me?" So David would not move the ark of the Lord with him into the City of David; but David took it aside into the house of Obed-Edom the Gittite. The ark of the Lord remained in the house of Obed-Edom the Gittite three months. And the Lord blessed Obed-Edom and all his household.

Now it was told King David, saying, "The Lord has blessed the house of Obed-Edom and all that belongs to him, because of the ark of God." So David went and brought up the ark of God from the house of Obed-Edom to the City of David with gladness."

II Samuel 6:1-12

David was bringing the Ark of God back to the house of God with Uzzah and Ahio. In the process of bringing the Ark back, Uzzah touched the Ark, the holy thing of God, and was killed instantly by God for his mistake. David became frightened and decided he no longer wanted to carry the holy Ark of God back to the house of God. He decided to leave it in the care of Obed-Edom. David left it in his care because he knew that Obed-Edom reverenced the things of God. Obed-Edom was a Levite assigned as a gatekeeper or doorkeeper for the Ark of the Lord (*I Chronicles 15:24*). In choosing the home of Obed-Edom, David made a calculated decision to leave the ark in the guardianship of someone specific. It was in the care of one of many gatekeepers who knew and understood the significance of guarding and protecting the holiness of the Ark. Obed-Edom knew the importance of guarding and protecting that which was holy and sacred.

The Word of God lets us know that the Ark of the Lord stayed in the care of Obed-Edom for three months. During those three months, the Lord blessed him and his entire household. When David heard that Obed-Edom and his whole household was being blessed, he immediately recognized and discerned that it was because Obed-Edom was being a dedicated and devoted gatekeeper of the Ark. David then decided it was time to bring the Ark to the City of David. By following the due order and the original intent of God, David was now able to accomplish in his second attempt what he had not been able to complete in his first. David wisely gave the assignment to carry and relocate the holy and sacred vessel of God to the chosen and ordained gatekeepers of the Ark. God was glorified in this second attempt because the Ark of God was given the due reverence and honor that God had instructed in His Word.

First, if you want to see the fullness of the Glory of the Lord, you must institute a pure worship in the house. Institute a worship that truly magnifies and glorifies the Lord. A performance-based worship will not do. Just as David worshiped the Lord with his whole body, soul and spirit when the Ark of God returned to its ordained place, so should we render the same worship. Second, God is looking for houses that are committed to protecting His glory at any cost. God is looking for His gatekeepers to come into alignment and to position themselves for their assignment.

NEW WINESKIN, NEW MINDSET

As I bring this book to a close, allow me to state the following; new wineskins are emerging that will be sensitive to the outpouring and creativity that the Holy Spirit is releasing in this hour. This will necessitate new mindsets that are concerned more with guarding and ensuring that norms of the past are not absorbed into these new structures by default. These new mindsets will not be rigid, but will be open for discussion and the gathering of needed materials and information relevant to carrying out their assignments. Collaboration will be a key component as these wineskins are integrated into daily living, as opposed to a separate institution where people attend weekly. It will not function independently; rather it will actively be a vital source of wisdom and direction for individuals and for agencies.

In conclusion, as we came into each gate, we found the Lord Jesus Christ. At the entry of each of these gates, we are able to see a different dimension of Him and His call to the Church of the Living God. We are able to discern the mysteries of His desire for the Body of Christ. As we have explored each of these gates, we are now better equipped to prevent the gates of hell from prevailing in our lives and in our ministries.